Lecture Notes
in Business Information Processing

366

More information about this series at http://www.springer.com/series/7911

Robert Pergl · Eduard Babkin ·
Russell Lock · Pavel Malyzhenkov ·
Vojtěch Merunka (Eds.)

Enterprise and Organizational Modeling and Simulation

15th International Workshop, EOMAS 2019, Held at CAiSE 2019
Rome, Italy, June 3–4, 2019
Selected Papers

 Springer

Editors
Robert Pergl (iD)
Czech Technical University in Prague
Prague 6, Czech Republic

Russell Lock (iD)
Loughborough University
Loughborough, UK

Vojtěch Merunka (iD)
Czech Technical University in Prague
Prague 1, Czech Republic

Eduard Babkin (iD)
Higher School of Economics
National Research University
Nizhny Novgorod, Russia

Pavel Malyzhenkov (iD)
Higher School of Economics
National Research University
Nizhny Novgorod, Russia

ISSN 1865-1348   ISSN 1865-1356 (electronic)
Lecture Notes in Business Information Processing
ISBN 978-3-030-35645-3   ISBN 978-3-030-35646-0 (eBook)
https://doi.org/10.1007/978-3-030-35646-0

This Springer imprint is published by the registered company Springer Nature Switzerland AG
The registered company address is: Gewerbestrasse 11, 6330 Cham, Switzerland

Preface

The International Workshop on Enterprise and Organizational Modeling and Simulation (EOMAS) represents a forum where researchers and practitioners exchange and mutually enrich their views, approaches, and obtain results in the field of enterprise engineering and enterprise architecture. The most valuable asset of every conference and workshop is its community. The community of EOMAS is small, but it consists of founding members, long-term contributors, and every year it attracts new innovative participants. This year, EOMAS reached its 15th edition and took place in Rome, Italy, during June 3–4, 2019.

Traditionally, we can offer a balanced assortment of papers addressing formal foundations of enterprise modeling and simulation, conceptual modeling approaches, higher-level insights and applications bringing novel ideas to traditional approaches, as well as new emerging trends. In this post-proceedings you may find the selected papers. Out of 24 submitted papers, 12 were accepted for publication as full papers and for oral presentation, and each paper was carefully selected, reviewed, and revised. In additional to this we reflected on the interest of last year's invited workshop on usability and invited the experts to make a sequel. You can find a short report in this issue.

This year, we included a novel outlet of Master and Doctoral Consortium, which attracted young talent to present their work. The presented work was then discussed, and feedback, advice, and encouragement was given. We were really surprised by the relevance, methodological quality, and results of their work – you may find their contributions on our website https://eomas-workshop.org.

We would like to express our sincere thanks to the entire EOMAS community: the authors, the Program Committee and the CAiSE organizers, the chairs for their enthusiasm and devotion, as well as all participants for their contributions. We look forward to the 16th edition of EOMAS!

June 2019

Robert Pergl
Eduard Babkin
Russell Lock
Pavel Malyzhenkov
Vojtěch Merunka

A Little Semi-round Retrospective

When we founded Sigmas (Special Interest Group on Modeling and Simulation) at the Association for Information Systems and its EOMAS workshop 15 years ago, under the leadership of Professor Joseph Barjis, this was the time of the final penetration of object-oriented paradigm into the area of building large software applications. Indeed, software analysis and design methods at that time had already assumed that software engineering processes begin with the description of requirements, but finding, verifying, and validating these requirements was considered as something that did not belong to software engineering techniques, because the software engineer must get it ready from other specialists. However, we have learned from our experience that this is not an accurate statement and that the requirements engineering must be part of software engineering, more specifically that software engineering has an essential intersection with business engineering and management consulting. Over the past years, the importance of this kind of analysis and prototyping of information systems grew as compared with the writing program code. Also, agile methods do not even assume that the requirements are accurately identified at the begin of the software development life cycle.

We are also delighted that in our workshop various innovative approaches have come into play, which later became asked at large conferences, but at the time of their beginning, they would probably not have the chance to be accepted elsewhere than in the EOMAS community. Our workshop should maintain this feature for the future and remain a platform for communication, inspiration, and collaboration of new ideas. In most countries, including mine, publications in peer-reviewed journals are more valued than publications at conferences of our type. However, it is a big problem for young scientists who cannot start to write journal articles without previous contact with the expert community. Our workshop is designed especially for them.

Dear friends, 15 great years of our workshop have passed, and there is a future ahead of us with new challenges. The dominance of Java has been declining already for many years, and new programming languages and new programming paradigms have come to the scene, in which return the spirit of the old ideas of Smalltalk, object databases, and other nearly forgotten technologies. Also, the declarative and other non-imperative styles of programming are no longer just an exciting toy but are becoming a practical technology, thanks to the growing performance of today's computers. We are interested in metamodeling and ontologies and augmentation of software engineering to the higher spheres of abstraction closer to classical philosophical thinking. Today's business consultants already use CASE tools and business-process simulators. This confirms the need for our workshop. Thank you all very much for the past 15 years of EOMAS workshop. Let us look into its future with great hope.

June 2019   Vojtěch Merunka

Organization

EOMAS 2019 was organized by the Department of Software Engineering, Czech Technical University in Prague, in cooperation with CAISE 2019 and CIAO! Enterprise Engineering Network.

Executive Committee

General Chair

Robert Pergl — Czech Technical University in Prague, Praha, Czech Republic

Program Chairs

Eduard Babkin — National Research University Higher School of Economics, Nizhny Novgorod, Russia
Russell Lock — Loughborough University, Loughborough, UK
Pavel Malyzhenkov — National Research University Higher School of Economics, Nizhny Novgorod, Russia
Vojtech Merunka — Czech Technical University in Prague, Praha, Czech Republic

Program Committee

David Aveiro — Madeira University, Portugal
Eduard Babkin — National Research University Higher School of Economics in Nizhni Novgorod, Russia
Joseph Barjis — San Jose State University, USA
Anna Bobkowska — Gdansk University of Technology, Poland
Alexander Bock — University of Duisburg-Essen, Germany
Mahmoud Boufaida — Mentouri University of Constantine, Algeria
Peter de Bruyn — University of Antwerp, Belgium
Simona Colucci — Politecnico di Bari, Italy
Francesco M. Donini — Università della Tuscia, Italy
Samuel Fosso Wamba — Toulouse Business School, France
Sergio Guerreiro — Instituto Superior Tecnico, University of Lisbon, Portugal
Frantisek Hunka — University of Ostrava, Czech Republic
Dmitry Kudryavtsev — Graduate School of Management, St. Petersburg University, Russia
Alexei Lapouchnian — University of Toronto, Canada
Russell Lock — Loughborough University, UK

Contents

Invited Workshop Notes

Conceptual Modelling

Designing an Ontology for Semantic Integration of Various Conceptual Models

Marek Suchánek(✉) 📷

Faculty of Information Technology, Czech Technical University in Prague,
16000 Prague 6, Czech Republic
marek.suchanek@fit.cvut.cz

Abstract. Ontologies and conceptual modelling are very close areas in software engineering. This paper is focused on initial steps towards the integration of conceptual models by the foundation of Ontology for Conceptual Models Integration to capture the knowledge about various conceptual modelling languages, including process, event, and object-role modelling. It is based on previous work in this area and has an ambitious goal to allow semantic integration of conceptual models made in different languages to cover more aspects and details of the problem domain. The presented contribution consists of the related work research, the initial ontology designed to be easily extensible, and related ideas for future work based on this foundation. We foresee this ontology to help also with using various conceptual models to create complete, consistent, and requisite software implementation in an automated way.

Keywords: Ontology · Conceptual modelling · Integration · Mapping

1 Introduction

Conceptual modelling is a discipline and activity used for describing a part of reality called problem domain (e.g., systems, environments, and organizations) in order to promote the understanding and communication between people [21]. When we understand a domain, we can improve it or support it efficiently, for example, by developing and incorporating software applications. There are many languages for modelling a domain, and there is definitely not a single correct way in choosing the language, similarly to programming languages [5]. Different languages are focused on different aspects of a domain (structure, processes, responsibilities, communication, etc.) and thus have certain advantages and disadvantages regarding a specific use case.

Although the modelling languages are more or less focus on different aspects or model the same aspects differently to enhance or align its usability, there are overlaps and connections in concepts and semantics [5]. Example of such connection can be nicely visible on models of the Unified Modelling Language (UML), where models relations between model are straightforward, for example, use case fulfilling a requirement, or object of a class from class diagram participating in

© Springer Nature Switzerland AG 2019
R. Pergl et al. (Eds.): EOMAS 2019, LNBIP 366, pp. 3–17, 2019.
https://doi.org/10.1007/978-3-030-35646-0_1

sequence behaviour model [23]. Such links are across other modelling languages as well. Using the links, we can interconnect the knowledge about the domain, improve understanding of it, and also translate between modelling languages – directly or interactively if personal decisions have to be made.

For the interconnection of models, we need to semantically integrate the languages, i.e., find and describe the overlaps and links. Semantic integration is a well-known process of interrelating information, and ontology mapping can be used for this purpose [14]. Ontologies are in information technologies are used for representing and storing knowledge using the formal encoding of taxonomies, structure of entities (nouns), and relations between them (verbs). There are already some works that encode modelling languages using their metamodels in the Web Ontology Language (OWL) as we will show in Sect. 2. Having OWL ontologies for various languages and then do ontology mapping seems a possible way of contributing to this area of research.

First, in Sect. 2, we briefly introduced used terminology of conceptual modelling; then we summarise related work in conceptual modelling and ontology mapping that will be used as a foundation for this work. In Sect. 3, we propose our solution to semantic integration of various conceptual models generically using ontology mapping, so it is applicable for any modelling language now or in the future. Section 4 contains the evaluation of our contribution and its possibilities of use based on the previous comprehensive description. Finally, Sect. 5 contains proposals of possibilities for further research in this area.

2   Related Work and Terminology

This section introduces basic terminology from conceptual modelling and ontology to understand and grasp the topic correctly. Then we briefly describe similar attempts to our topic and related work that we can use for our goals. It is further used to design our own solution.

2.1   Conceptual Modelling

As the *conceptual modelling*, we understand, according to [21], as "the activity of formally describing some aspects of the physical and social world around us for purposes of understanding and communication". This definition covers not only the structural modelling of entities, their attributes, and relationships with possible constraints but also processes or even social aspects such as responsibilities or intentions. Thus, in this paper, we do not make a distinction between structural, process or other models on the conceptual level.

Although the primary purpose of conceptual modelling is not strictly related to software engineering, it is often used in it to design software systems according to requirements of a well-described domain. There are various languages for conceptual modelling that are focused on specific aspects. For structural modelling, the study [28] shows that ontology-driven languages such as OntoUML [11] is better to use over traditional approaches with UML or ER models. Slightly other approach is taken in Object-Role Modeling (ORM) that is focused on modelling facts and their roles in relations between them [12].

Facts-oriented is also part of the Design & Engineering Methodology for Organizations (DEMO) that focuses on transactions, i.e., production and coordination, in organisations and provides multiple consistent models to cover structures, processes, and action rules [7]. For purely process modelling, aside to well-known BPMN and some UML models, there is also Business Objects Relation Modelling (BORM) based on the object-oriented paradigm and formalism of communicating finite machines [15].

2.2 Ontology Mapping, Alignment, and Matching

Ontology matching, sometimes called ontology alignment, is the process of finding correspondences between concepts in two or more ontologies. A set of such correspondences can be described with a term *alignment*. In the past, it was mainly used for integrating databases or software applications with different vocabularies. There are three dimensions by which we can match terms in ontologies: syntactic, external, and semantic [26].

When we have two ontologies with their sets of classes, relations, individuals, data types, and values, we can match them using inter-ontology relationships. A single matching is given by two terms that match and the similarity measure, which is a value between 0 and 1. A pair of those two terms from a single matching is called mapping [26].

For mapping multiple ontologies, you can map them in pairs (each-to-each), or have one particular ontology as a central point to which is each ontology mapped. The second option is what we want to do in our work. An important note is that we do not want to lose important information about mapping by using just similarity measure but to capture what semantic difference is between terms even if it is very slight.

2.3 Description-Logics Based Ontologies

Formal specifications are used to represent some knowledge in a well-defined way another family with this common goal is description logic (DL). Problem domains can be described using DL languages, which can use various description logics: general, spatial, temporal, spatiotemporal, and fuzzy [1]. DL is tightly connected to ontologies in software engineering, for example, and more specifically, with the Web Ontology Language (OWL), since version 2 defined by W3C consortium.

A model can be then described using OWL, where *classes* correspond to DL *concepts*, *properties* to DL *roles*, and *individuals* are the same. An OWL ontology is usually used in semantic web technologies or to describe some data in RDF format and is compatible with RDF schemas. Thanks to its popularity over the recent years, tooling support is on a granular level and also allows visualisation. When compared to a graphical language it is more efficient to develop text-based OWL for versioning using tools like Git instead of storing models in XMI or as figures [10, 19].

2.4   Matching in OWL

Matching, as we already described, is used to interconnect ontologies with relationships of equivalence and similarity [26]. In OWL, there are already defined terms that can be used for matching ontologies [3]:

- `owl:equivalentClass` = a property for linking class descriptions that have the same intensional meaning and are not necessarily totally equivalent (which can be done with `owl:sameAs`).
- `owl:equivalentProperty` = a construct for stating that two properties have the same property extension, i.e., intensional meaning. Just as with `owl:equivalentClass`, totally equivalent property should be instead captured with `owl:sameAs`.
- `owl:sameAs` = a property for linking individuals with the same "identity". Similarly, there are also properties `owl:differentFrom` together with set-like `owl:AllDifferent` for different individuals.

   As those and also other exist [19], we should make use of those and do not "reinvent the wheel". OWL language is very expressive in this manner, and it can significantly help us with our task of semantic integration of various conceptual models.

2.5   Ontology for Conceptual Modelling

Very similar research to this has been done in [18], and we are highly inspired by it. The significant difference in their and our work lies in their main focus on structural aspects, i.e., its simplicity and actually mapping conceptual models into vocabularies with just types (i.e., classes or entities), qualities (i.e., attributes or properties), and relations. Also, they are focused on usability with Biomedical Informatics Grid and clinical models that limit the generality of the project.

   The other problem is that the ontology is not available any more, and the project seems abandoned. Our goal is to ensure future development of the ontology and not leaving it to disappear. As another inspiring part of this work, there are relations to terms in other upper ontologies such as BFO, SKOS, or IAO. That can even allow mappings between different ontologies and conceptual models as is done entirely in OntoUML modelling language [11].

2.6   Model Transformations

A lot of work in model transformations has been already done. First, in model-driven software engineering, there are many tools and ways of translating a conceptual model into (usually incomplete) implementation. The most known approach is Model Driven Architecture (MDA) by OMG where computation independent model (CIM) is transformed to platform independent model (PIM) and then to platform specific model (PSM) [27]. During the transformations, conceptual details can be lost, and implementation information is added.

Also, transformations between modelling languages and conceptual modelling to ontologies have been done as well. For example, [2] describes transformation of OntoUML to OWL and SWRL, similarly to [31] and [30] about UML to OWL transformation. OntoUML can also be transformed into the formal specification in language Alloy [4]. Such transformations are used often for increasing possibilities of the language, for example, transforming OntoUML to Alloy allows validation with mathematical reasoning and generation of instances which would be more complicated to reimplement purely for OntoUML.

2.7 Existing Ontologies for Modelling Languages

There are already existing ontologies that encode metamodels of modelling languages which is even more powerful than simple transformations of models into ontology. It allows matching of modelling languages and querying as well as it describes instances, i.e., models. One of many examples is [22] that encodes BPMN 2.0 into ontology as organised knowledge from more than 500 pages of the official specification. It provides annotations and information about BPMN but also enables validations of BPMN models.

2.8 Meta-modelling and MOF

The Meta-Object Facility (MOF) [24] is a standard by Object Management Group (OMG) used in model-driven engineering. It defines 4 levels wherein the top M3 level is provided with a meta-metamodel which conforms to itself and that can be used to build compliant metamodels on the M2 level for modelling languages, such as, UML metamodel. Then on the M1 level are the models made in the language defined by M2 metamodel, e.g., UML model. The M0 level is data level with real-world objects, i.e., model instances.

Some modelling languages and their metamodels are conformed with MOF and some, of course, are not. Sharing the meta-metamodel gives an advantage in the form of transformation possibilities or interconnecting knowledge between models that we want to achieve as well. Inspirations from MOF's M3 model and mapping it directly are essential to our work.

3 Our Approach

In this section, we propose and describe our initial ontology for the integration of various conceptual models though matching their metamodels. For that purpose, we highly gather inspirations from the discussed related work. Our goal is to develop a high-quality foundation of ontology that will be extended continually in the future rather than struggling with an enormous amount of different concepts from many modelling languages or developing totally new multi-aspect language as is often the case in contemporary software engineering. The re-use of concepts and ideas is the essence of our work together with abstractions and categorisations of those terms if applicable and needed.

3.1   General Requirements

First, we need to summarise what are the demands that need to be fulfilled. Such requirements are of two kinds. We want to develop an ontology that captures the knowledge of conceptual models. It means we want to extract higher-level terms, such as class, entity, relation, inheritance, and so on, used in various (commonly used) conceptual modelling languages, group them, and name the group within the ontology. Selected aspects (i.e., types of modelling) and modelling languages for our purpose are:

- Class-oriented modelling: UML Class Diagram, OntoUML, ER
- Fact-oriented modelling: ORM, DEMO
- Behavioural modelling: UML Activity Diagram, BPMN, BORM
- Instance-level modelling: UML Object Diagram.

As for the second kind of requirements, which we can call as in software engineering "non-functional" requirements, we narrow selection of technologies and architecture in order to be extensible and interoperable in the future development. Setting up and following such requirements should, for example, assure that our work will not end up unavailable like mentioned Conceptual Modelling Ontology from [18]. We will mainly focus on this using FAIR principles [29]:

- **Findable** = The ontology and related metadata should be publicly available in a repository that assures long-term storage, and persistent identifier (for example, DOI) will be assigned.
- **Accessible** = The ontology and metadata will be accessible using open and free protocol via the Internet from the public repository.
- **Interoperable** = The selected format to represent the ontology and metadata needs to be open and widely used, preferably standardised, and it should be clear how to use it.
- **Reusable** = The project should be released with a clear usage license, detailed provenance, and it should meet standards used in similar projects.

To fulfil most of these "non-functional" requirements, we will use a public GitHub repository, open Creative Commons license, and Zenodo service to assign persistent Digital Object Identifier (DOI) [25]. The repository will contain aside to the ontology description also files to clarifies its usage both human-readable and machine-actionable.

Another aspect is the quality and truthfulness of the ontology. The ontology must be, of course satisfiable, i.e., it is possible to instantiate the described model without any violation of specified rules. There are also measures of quality proposed by [16] in terms of syntax, (perceived) semantics, pragmatics, knowledge, social, physical, and language aspects. In order to achieve validity and completeness, which will be a long-term goal above the scope of this paper, everyone developing this ontology should take those quality aspects into account.

3.2   Technologies and Formats

Concerning the previously discussed requirements, we selected OWL format for implementing the ontology. It is standardised by OMG, has excellent tooling support, has advantages over RDF schemas or previously used frame languages [19]. The ultimate tool to work with ontologies that we will also use is Protégé, which is free and open-source [20]. For visualisations to explain the ontology in this paper, we will use a web-based visualisation tool called WebVOWL [17].

To describe the project, we will use a simple documentation HTML documentation for people as well as machines. It will contain metadata encoded using tool WIDOCO – a wizard for documenting ontologies [8]. The documentation will contain information about the ontology, its license, authors, and intended usage together with relevant references, including this paper. The OWL ontology will also be annotated using well-known Dublin Core standard [13].

3.3   Ontology for Conceptual Models Integration

In our ontology called *Ontology for Conceptual Models Integration* (OCMI), we gather key terms from various conceptual modelling languages as described in requirements. The highest level of classes consists of five terms: Entity, Event, Property, Relationship, and Participation. There are two more terms – Constraint and Instance – that are sort of "cross-cutting concerns" since they can be related to one of the previous four terms, for example, a constraint for a relationship or an instance of an entity. Thus, they have subclasses for each of them. The core is well visible in Fig. 1 made by WebVOWL tool.

Aside from classes, we defined also data and object properties based on the modelling languages analysis and conceptual modelling principles. The most basic example is that every Entity, Property, Relationship, and other have a name (e.g. entity "Person" or property "birthdate"). They also capture relations between our classes, for instance, that one entity constraint is related to some entities and that one entity can have multiple entity constraints. The core terms forming the "spine" of ontology are:

Entity. We call an *entity* the same things as is a *class* in UML and its profiles, a *fact* in ORM and DEMO and identically *entity* in the ER modelling. It is a structural pattern for its instances, i.e., it groups definitions of properties and relationships that the instances have in common. This is the core term of our ontology used when defining all others.

Event. *Event* is a subclass of an entity which is special in terms of its usage. It represents entity that occurs in time duration and has special relations and properties related to that fact, such as a trigger, input, and output. In process modelling, the equivalent naming is activity, transition, or task.

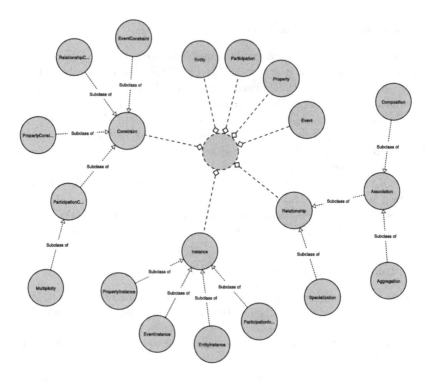

Fig. 1. WebVOWL visualisation of OCMI (core, details are collapsed)

Property. Commonly known *attributes*, *fields*, *trait*, or *quality* from conceptual modelling languages, we call a *property* definition of having a named feature. In the first version of ER modelling, this was captured by the special *has* relation, for example, "Car has a colour". It is important to mention here, that property has no type definition - we understand typing as kind of *constraint* which are defined later on.

Relationship. Aside from properties, an entity can have some *relationships* with other entities or itself. In conceptual models, there are relations, links, associations, and so on. We use the term relationship for any kind of connection between two (or more) entities. The entities are connected to relationship via special class *participation* to separate connection details. There are also subclasses of relationships such as *specialization*, *association*, or *aggregation*.

Participation. The *Participation* class serves to name and describe an relationship "end". It is better to separate details about a single connection of entity to a relationship from others, especially when a relationship can be (theoretically) between any number of entities. The main purpose is regarding the constraints.

Constraint. As being said, *constraint* realizes any sort of restriction of others in our ontology. We understand as a constraint multiplicity of relationship (more specifically participation of relationship), a stereotype of entity or relationship, specially named meta-attributes, but even datatype of property, and so on. There are subclasses of constraints for other classes and then special subclasses for widely used constraints in conceptual modelling.

Instance. From instance-level modelling, we got inspired and incorporated class *instance* for something called also *object* in the UML and its profiles. Instances of entities, relationships, participations, or properties (i.e., values) form an instance of a model and are related to its class.

The resulting ontology contains more terms and their properties than shown in Fig. 1 but those are collapsed and are less significant to be explicitly stated here. We expect that such lower-level terms and details might change over time but mentioned and critical seven of higher-level terms will be stable and provide a solid foundation.

3.4   Distribution

The ontology is published using GitHub repository, but we provide persistent links to the repository itself http://purl.org/ocmi and the latest OWL file http://purl.org/ocmi/ocmi.owl in the master branch. This mechanism of purl.org service [9] allows us to change the provider, owner, or name of the repository and keep the same URL as well as potentially change even the name of the ontology itself. The universal Creative Commons license CC0 (Public Domain) does not limit any use or distribution of the ontology [6]. The first starting release allowed to create a release with DOI using Zenodo that makes the ontology with specific versions simple to cite [25].

3.5   Relations with Upper Ontologies

As we developed an ontology of high-level terms of the conceptual modelling domain, it inevitably overlaps on semantic and maybe even syntactic level with upper (or foundational) ontologies. We selected some of the widely used upper ontologies: General Formal Ontology (GFO), Basic Formal Ontology (BFO), Unified Foundational Ontology (UFO), and Yet Another More Advanced Top-level Ontology (YAMATO), and compared classes in our ontology with theirs. The results are summarised in Table 1. The captured equivalences can also be described using `owl:equivalentClass` and are based on empirical observations of their use in multiple domain ontologies as well as its description in upper ontologies.

We matched terms with an elementary knowledge of selected ontologies, and it can be a source of other future discussions for improvements in our OCMI ontology. It is visible that no existing ontology perfectly matches our new one, but it can be mapped, often even with the partially identical terminology.

Table 1. Equivalent terms in the selected ontologies

OCMI	GFO	BFO	UFO	YAMATO
Entity	Entity	Entity	Universal	Entity
Event	SpaceTime	Occurent	Perdurant	Occurent
Relationship	Relator (only)	Relational quality	Relation	Relation
Participation	Relational role	N/A	N/A	N/A
Property	Property	Quality	Aspect/Quality	Property

4   Evaluation

The described *Ontology for Conceptual Models Integration* successfully fulfils the set initial requirements. First, it contains all essential terms used in the analysed modelling languages which enable future integrations on overlapping terms, encoding models using RDF and the ontology, and querying in a standard OWL way. Also, thanks to the selected standard OWL format, the ontology can be interconnected with existing OWL ontologies for conceptual modelling, and it is easily extensible.

4.1   Evolvability

As we already stated, our ontology presented in this paper is just an initial step, and the main advantage is within its ability to be continually improved in a crowd-sourced manner. Use of standard format, versioning, and overall design enable easy changes in the future without causing any ripple effects. The ontology maintainers can quickly review its distribution and licensing also allow anyone to contribute and the contributions. The team of maintainers can, over time, change based on proving expertise and ability to contribute regularly. Nevertheless, the main ideas and requirements given by this paper should remain the same.

4.2   Versatility

The contribution in the form of a single initial ontology based on conceptual modelling languages analysis can be marked as versatile. It uses only standard technologies and procedures; therefore, it has no other limitations than those set by the underlying technologies and human creativity. As the name states, the primary purpose is to integrate conceptual models, but it can be used for modelling itself or as an upper ontology to other ontologies. Also, usage as a descriptor to generate software entities can be done as well. It is all achieved by its simplicity that can, of course, disappear in the future as the ontology will get mature.

4.3 Possibilities for Adoption

Thanks to its versatility mentioned above, there is plenty of opportunities for the use of the Ontology for Conceptual Models Integration. First, as it is standard OWL ontology, it can be freely used in other ontologies that describe conceptual modelling languages (or are generic upper ontologies) with use of equivalence or subtype relations similarly to what we have shown in Table 1. Such "crowd-sourced" use would specify the mappings for integration itself.

Then, integration can be realised using OWL queries on the lower level of domain models. Another option is to develop a framework that takes the ontology, mapped modelling languages and upper ontologies, a domain model and provides many options for results such as:

– manipulation (i.e., queries) of model composed of multiple conceptual models from the input,
– transformations of models between modelling languages,
– consistency checks for multiple models,
– template-based generating documentation, statistics, and visualisations from models.

There can be many implementations of such a framework using different technologies. The ontology defines very high-level terminology of conceptual modelling with intentions but not specifications nor limitation of its use. However, the core idea will persist – a well-defined combination of conceptual modelling languages to describe a problem domain instead of developing new languages.

4.4 Availability and FAIRness

We published our work within the public Git repository and created a persistent URL using purl.org service, which assures long-term availability. On top of that, the repository also allows releases with DOI using Zenodo service. Development of the ontology is simplified thanks to the regular Git workflow with branches, tags, and forks. Due to permissive licensing, anyone can adjust the ontology or contribute to it.

Finally, the documentation on how to use, extend, and integrate the ontology is provided directly in the repository together with project-related metadata in both human-readable and machine-actionable format. With all of this, the ontology is ready for further elaboration and usage to integrate conceptual models on the semantic level. Use of standard formats, open access, and metadata as described in requirements makes this project FAIR.

5 Future Work and Research Ideas

While developing the ontology and studying related work, we have encountered several challenges and possibilities for future research. Potential further steps after this research are briefly described in this section.

5.1 More Modelling Languages

The most obvious way to continue in this work is to describe more modelling languages using our ontology. For higher efficiency of the process, prioritisation of languages should take place. Incorporating modelling languages that already have some published and available OWL description should be more comfortable and faster to adopt with ontology alignment instead of thoroughly research the meta-model and encode it. On the other hand, widely-used languages should be preferred to incorporate over less-used even if having OWL specification.

The primary purpose of doing this is, of course, to cover more aspects of a domain and to provide more ways of modelling that can be plugged together. There is also the second advantage in the form of improving the ontology for integration. When we encounter a modelling language that has some constructs which cannot be adequately captured with the ontology, or the loss of information is too high, an improvement of the ontology should be made to increase its expressiveness. Important is to still stay on a very generic level and do not dive into describing too detailed concepts that would prevent a proper mapping.

5.2 Formal Specifications

Aside to incorporating more languages for conceptual modelling, the scope of languages can be broadened, and other forms of a domain description could be added. Formal specification, for example, Alloy, OCL, or algebraic specifications (Maude, CASL, etc.), are an essential way how to capture specific details of a domain or a system that are usually not possible to encode in graphical conceptual modelling languages. Importance of those models is mainly in its possibility of mathematical reasoning and proving correctness or broad validation options in terms of automatically generating instances.

Meta-models of languages for formal specifications differ in many aspects; however, since they are often used as complements to conceptual models for mission-critical parts of a domain, overlaps and interconnections must be present. Further research could enhance the ontology to allow adopting formal specification languages and enable its symbiotic connection to various conceptual models in a simple way.

5.3 Similarity and Expressiveness of Modelling Languages

Since we can match various conceptual modelling languages using a common ontology, we can also evaluate how are these languages similar, i.e., how much they cover the same aspects of a domain in the same scope. Knowing easily how expressive is each modelling language concerning particular domain aspect or aspects should help with deciding what language is suitable to be used for a description of a domain based on requirements and expectations. Moreover, when it is known which other languages are highly compatible (i.e., can create synergic models) – a whole suite of suitable languages for given problem domain could be decided with higher quality.

5.4   Implementation Models and Transformations

Formal specifications are closer to a mathematical or programming-like description of a domain. Another natural broadening of the ontology scope would be covering implementation models. It should allow transforming a set of conceptual models and possibly formal specifications into a set of implementation models able to be used for generating adequate software application. Of course, such transformation is not straightforward, since between conceptual and implementation levels are gaps as technical details are missing in conceptual models but contain other details that are omitted in implementations.

An existing approach used in MDA well describe such transformation and is verified by practice. The novelty brought by our ontology would be in seamlessly using multiple different models that cover more aspects, and thus hypothetically more accurate implementation can be generated. This topic of all other mentioned here represents, in our opinion, the most complicated challenge, as well as the most significant benefit.

6   Conclusion

In this paper, we presented our initial approach to semantically integrate various conceptual models made in different modelling languages with the use of current ontology technologies. Our work that was profoundly influenced by interesting but discontinued *Conceptual Modelling Ontology (CMO)* [18] and Meta-Object Facility collects knowledge from different approaches to conceptual modelling and provides a way how to map them together in order to allow a description of a problem domain from diverse aspects. The ontology is easily extensible and can be continually improved when incorporating new modelling languages. We hope that our contribution will be used as a foundation to further research and application in practice to help in conceptual modelling and model-driven development of software applications.

Acknowledgments. This research was supported by the grant of Czech Technical University in Prague No. SGS17/211/OHK3/3T/18.

References

1. Baader, F., Horrocks, I., Lutz, C., Sattler, U.: Introduction to Description Logic. Cambridge University Press, Cambridge (2017)
2. Barcelos, P.P.F., dos Santos, V.A., Silva, F.B., Monteiro, M.E., Garcia, A.S.: An automated transformation from OntoUML to OWL and SWRL. Ontobras **1041**, 130–141 (2013)
3. Bechhofer, S., et al.: OWL: Web Ontology Language Reference. W3C recommendation 10(02) (2004)
4. Braga, B.F., Almeida, J.P.A., Guizzardi, G., Benevides, A.B.: Transforming OntoUML into alloy: towards conceptual model validation using a lightweight formal method. Innov. Syst. Softw. Eng. **6**(1–2), 55–63 (2010)

5. Brodie, M.L., Mylopoulos, J., Schmidt, J.W.: On Conceptual Modelling: Perspectives from Artificial Intelligence, Databases, and Programming Languages. Springer, New York (2012)

6. Creative Commons: CC0 1.0 Universal (2019). https://creativecommons.org/publicdomain/zero/1.0/deed.cs

7. Dietz, J.L.: Towards a discipline of organisation engineering. Eur. J. Oper. Res. **128**(2), 351–363 (2001)

8. Garijo, D.: WIDOCO: a wizard for documenting ontologies. In: d'Amato, C., et al. (eds.) ISWC 2017. LNCS, vol. 10588, pp. 94–102. Springer, Cham (2017). https://doi.org/10.1007/978-3-319-68204-4_9

9. Graham, M.: Persistent URL Service, purl.org, Now Run by the Internet Archive. blog.archive.org (2016)

10. Grau, B.C., Horrocks, I., Motik, B., Parsia, B., Patel-Schneider, P., Sattler, U.: OWL 2: the next step for OWL. Web Semant. Sci. Serv. Agents World Wide Web **6**(4), 309–322 (2008)

11. Guizzardi, G.: Ontological Foundations for Structural Conceptual Models. Centre for Telematics and Information Technology, Telematica Instituut, University of Twente, Enschede, The Netherlands (2005). http://doc.utwente.nl/50826/1/thesis_Guizzardi.pdf

12. Halpin, T.: Object-Role Modeling Fundamentals: A Practical Guide to Data Modeling with ORM. Technics Publications, LLC, Basking Ridge (2015)

13. Dublin Core Metadata Initiative and others: Dublin core metadata element set, version 1.1 (2012)

14. Kalfoglou, Y., et al. (eds.) Semantic Interoperability and Integration, no. 04391 in Dagstuhl Seminar Proceedings. Internationales Begegnungs- und Forschungszentrum für Informatik (IBFI), Schloss Dagstuhl, Germany, Dagstuhl, Germany (2005)

15. Knott, R., Merunka, V., Polák, J.: The BORM method: a third generation object-oriented methodology. In: Management of the Object-Oriented Development Process. IGI Global (2005)

16. Krogstie, J., Lindland, O.I., Sindre, G.: Defining quality aspects for conceptual models. In: Falkenberg, E.D., Hesse, W., Olivé, A. (eds.) Information System Concepts. IAICT, pp. 216–231. Springer, Boston, MA (1995). https://doi.org/10.1007/978-0-387-34870-4_22

17. Lohmann, S., Link, V., Marbach, E., Negru, S.: WebVOWL: web-based visualization of ontologies. In: Lambrix, P., et al. (eds.) EKAW 2014. LNCS (LNAI), vol. 8982, pp. 154–158. Springer, Cham (2015). https://doi.org/10.1007/978-3-319-17966-7_21

18. McCusker, J.P., Luciano, J.S., McGuinness, D.L.: Towards an ontology for conceptual modeling. In: Proceedings of the 2nd International Conference on Biomedical Ontology, Buffalo, NY, USA, 26–30 July 2011 (2011). http://ceur-ws.org/Vol-833/paper25.pdf

19. McGuinness, D.L., Van Harmelen, F., et al.: OWL: Web Ontology Language Overview. W3C recommendation 10(10), 2004 (2004)

20. Musen, M.A., et al.: The Protégé project: a look back and a look forward. AI Matters **1**(4), 4 (2015)

21. Mylopoulos, J.: Conceptual Modelling and Telos. Conceptual Modelling, Databases, and CASE: An Integrated View of Information System Development, pp. 49–68. Wiley, New York (1992)

22. Natschläger, C.: Towards a BPMN 2.0 ontology. In: Dijkman, R., Hofstetter, J., Koehler, J. (eds.) BPMN 2011. LNBIP, vol. 95, pp. 1–15. Springer, Heidelberg (2011). https://doi.org/10.1007/978-3-642-25160-3_1

23. Object Management Group (OMG): OMG unified modeling language, v. 2.5. Technical report (2015). http://www.omg.org/spec/UML/2.5/PDF

24. OMG: OMG Meta Object Facility (MOF) Core Specification, Version 2.5.1 (2013). http://www.omg.org/spec/MOF/2.5.1

25. Potter, M., Smith, T.: Making code citable with zenodo and github. Software Sustainibility Institute (2015)

26. Shvaiko, P., Euzenat, J.: Ontology matching: state of the art and future challenges. IEEE Trans. Knowl. Data Eng. **25**(1), 158–176 (2013)

27. Truyen, F.: The Fast Guide to Model Driven Architecture - The basics of Model Driven Architecture (2006). http://www.omg.org/mda/mda_files/Cephas_MDA_Fast_Guide.pdf

28. Verdonck, M., Gailly, F., Pergl, R., Guizzardi, G., Martins, B., Pastor, O.: Comparing traditional conceptual modeling with ontology-driven conceptual modeling: an empirical study. Information Systems (2018). http://dx.doi.org/10.1016/j.is.2018.11.009

29. Wilkinson, M.D., et al.: The FAIR Guiding Principles for Scientific Data Management and Stewardship. Scientific Data **3** (2016)

30. Zedlitz, J., Jörke, J., Luttenberger, N.: From UML to OWL 2. In: Lukose, D., Ahmad, A.R., Suliman, A. (eds.) KTW 2011. CCIS, vol. 295, pp. 154–163. Springer, Heidelberg (2012). https://doi.org/10.1007/978-3-642-32826-8_16

31. Zedlitz, J., Luttenberger, N.: Transforming between UML conceptual models and OWL 2 ontologies. In: Terra Cognita 2012 Workshop, vol. 6, p. 15 (2012)

Conceptual Normalisation in Software Engineering

Martin Molhanec[✉]

Faculty of Electrical Engineering, Department of Electrotechnology,
Czech Technical University, Prague, Czech Republic
molhanec@fel.cvut.cz

Abstract. This article argues the necessity of conceptual normalisation in software engineering and data development. Moreover, it aims to put a basis for formal definitions of conceptual normal forms. The Author's approach is ontologically based exploiting an axiom of non-redundancy of the Real World. Further, the Author also shows how relational and object normalisation are connected with a conceptual one. In the end, the Author argues for herein proposed ideas and definitions.

Keywords: Data normalisation · Conceptual normal forms · Object normal forms · Relational normal forms · Conceptual modelling · Data modelling · Ontology

1 Introduction

This article is engaged with the issue of conceptual normalisation. The Author has been concerned with this issue for many years and published his ideas in the past years at different scientific events, for example, at EOMAS international workshop [1–3], ISD (Information System Development) conference [4] and, as well as many local Czech conferences and seminars; we afford to refer only a few of them [5–7], so this article is one of many of such disseminating the Author's opinions in the wider scope of international as well as local expert community engaging in conceptual, object and data modelling. The Author hopes that this contribution can be a good starting point for a more extensive discussion about these very interesting and serious problems.

The rest of this paper is organised as follows. Next, in Sect. 2, we start by motivating the need for conceptual normalisation. Section 3 introduces our presumptions and approach. After that, Sect. 4 gives the results of our work, i.e., the proposal of definitions, formal and informal, of four conceptual normal forms, and finally, Sect. 5 summarises the paper, suggests improvements and discusses future directions for research.

2 Motivation and Problem Statement

The paradigm of relational normalisation (1st to 3rd normal forms and others that are not so common such as BNCF, etc.) is commonly taught in university courses in the field

© Springer Nature Switzerland AG 2019
R. Pergl et al. (Eds.): EOMAS 2019, LNBIP 366, pp. 18–28, 2019.
https://doi.org/10.1007/978-3-030-35646-0_2

of database theory and design. There are no doubts about the usefulness and advisability of it. We can refer, for example, the works of Codd [8–10] among others. Regrettably, there are many opinions about the nonsensicality of the normalisation principle in the field of an object-oriented paradigm given that object-oriented databases do not use the concept of primary and foreign keys. This is false in the opinion of the Author.

It is true that issues of right design of data models have been discussed of the 70s starting with a well-known article by Chen [11]. Particular attention to this issue is paid by fact-based modelling approach, for example, in [12] and [13], among others. Nevertheless, the Author's modern-day approach based on ontology theory and covering conceptual, object and relation modelling paradigm is in some respect different from them, according to the opinion of the Author.

Another reason for conceptual normalisation is a need to retain a consistency of gradual models during MDD (Model Driven Development) transformations (see, for instance, [14]).

We argued that the need for object normalisation arises from the same reasons as for relational normalisation, i.e., from the needfulness of elimination of redundancy from our data. The employment of primary and foreign keys in definitions of relational normalisation is, thus, to implement the process of relational normalisation for relational databases. So, for the definition of object normalisation, we need a different tool for our endeavour.

This approach is also supported by many experts, for example, Ambler [15], Nootenboom [16], Yonghui [17], Tari [18] and Khodorkovsky [19], among others. A brief description of approaches of all these authors is included in Molhanec and Merunka [20]. It is clear that all these authorities agree on the necessity of object normalisation, but still, there exist some issues to resolve, such as:

- *There are no definitively and generally accepted definitions of object normal forms.*
- *Most of the authors have a problem with replacing the concept of relational keys with other correct concept in the definition of object normalisation.*
- *It is not clear if the same count of normal forms exists in the object area as well as in the relational area.*

3   Presumptions and Our Approach

We start this section with the following, in our view, a fundamental presumption that the relational and object models are specialisations of the more common and high-level conceptual model, and simultaneously, that these models there are not a sub-type of each other. For that account, we defend, that both the relational and object normalisations are the specialisation of the conceptual normalisation as well. This simple but basic assertion is concisely shown in following Fig. 1.

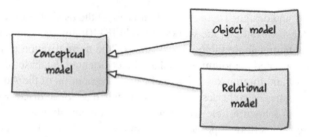

Fig. 1. Conceptual, relational and object models

This basic idea (presumption, conjecture) can be defined more formally as follows:

Conjecture (relational and object models inherit from a conceptual model):
Let *CM*, *RM* and *OM* be *Conceptual Model*, *Relational Model* and *Object Model* respectively. We assert that the following is true:

$$(RM \sqsubseteq CM) \wedge (OM \sqsubseteq CM) \wedge (RM \not\sqsubseteq OM) \wedge (OM \not\sqsubseteq RM) \tag{1}$$

Here it should be mentioned the misguided argument which frequently arises in the course of the conversation about the necessity of object normalisation and differences between the object and relational approaches.

> *"The object approach has not and does not need any primary and foreign keys, therefore it is better than the relational approach and its normalisation is thus nonsense."*

This argument, along with the idea surrounding normalisation as something that relates to the primary and foreign keys, implicates an idea that normalisation in the area of an object-oriented paradigm is nonsense. However, as previously mentioned, the normalisation paradigm is not about the keys, because the keys in the relational area are only the proper devices that define the normal forms, but normalisation is essentially about redundancy which rises from the absence of redundancy in the Real World around us, in the sense of work [21].

In the sequel, we introduce some conjectures, definitions and lemmas needed to build up our approach of conceptual normalisation and conceptual normal forms as well.

3.1 Uniqueness and Identity

Our approach conforms to Quine's dictum *"no entity without identity"* [22]. The concepts of uniqueness and identity of objects in Real World are essential for the Author because that are very closely connected with the principle of non-redundancy of Real World as well as with the definitions of the conceptual normal forms discussed and defended by us. Accordingly to Guizzardi [23] and Herre [24] we may to formally formulate a conjecture below. The formalisation is based on intensional sortal modal logics (i.e., intensional modal logics with quantification restricted by sortal) with minimum additions to it as used in [25].

Conjecture (identity and uniqueness): Let RW be Real World, and, x, y are objects of that. Next, let the predicate *id* denote identity. We assert that the following is true:

$$\forall (x \in RW)\square \exists id(x) \tag{2}$$

$$\forall (x \in RW)(y \in RW)(id(x) = id(y) \rightarrow x \equiv y) \tag{3}$$

Simply put, for all objects of Real World, there exists necessarily an output value of identity function; as well as if values of identity function of two objects are equal, then these objects are identical.

It is clear that these assertions are fundamental. We cannot predicate that any natural world objects have any real internal identifiers. Any unique identification of an object such as a serial number is an artificial property created by a human being for the intention of creating a unique identification. However, the majority of natural world objects do not have such identification at all. However, all real objects have their physical identity. Abstract objects, such as an invoice in an information system, must always have an artificial identifier. In any case, we only deal with objects that can be clearly distinguished from each other at a given time in our Real World. Whether any way.

3.2   The Conceptual Object and Its Features

This section introduces the concept of the property of a conceptual object as well as some other essential definitions, lemmas and theorems employed in subsequent sections of this work. We start by giving a simple definition of property of the object.

Definition (property): *A property is a particular characteristic of an object having a value.* $\tag{4}$

An example of such a property could be colour or age. Then, the property can also be a set. We use our term in the same sense as Guizzardi and Wagner use the term intrinsic moment in [26]. They claim that:

> *"Intrinsic Moments: qualities such as a color, a weight, an electric charge, a circular shape; modes such as a thought, a skill, a belief, an intention, a headache, as well as dispositions such as the refrangibility property of light rays, or the disposition of a magnetic material to attract a metallic object."*

Thus, a property is a particular abstraction of an object's characterisation, a constituent of its intension and distinguishable or perceivable by a human being.

Lemma (property uniqueness): Let O be an object, and, p, q, be properties of it, and, the predicate *in* denotes a set of all properties of that object, and, predicate *cm* denotes a conceptual meaning of that. We assert that the following is true:

$$\forall (p \in in(O))(q \in in(O))(cm(p) = cm(q) \rightarrow p \equiv q) \tag{5}$$

It is to say if two properties of the object have the same conceptual meaning, thus must be the same. Conversely, the set of object properties is unique in the context of it.

This lemma can be explained as follows. A car has only one colour property. Of course, the colour of the car body is separate property to the colour of the car's chassis. Therefore, these two colours are two different properties. Next, a person has only one age property, denominated 'age', and so on. We can prove the property, and the result is that the property is a concept as well. In other words, a real car does not have two colours, and a person does not have two ages at the same time.

The following theorems proposed by the Author relate to object properties as well.

Theorem (conceptual property atomicity): Let P_O be a set of all properties of an object O, and, p be a property of it, and, c be a concept, and, finally, predicate cm denotes a conceptual meaning of its argument. We assert that the following is true:

$$\forall p \in P_O \rightarrow \neg \exists c \sqsubseteq cm(p) \tag{6}$$

In other words, a conceptual meaning of any object property is not dividable, i.e., object property is atomic. If we need to work with a part of it, in the sense of conceptual meaning, the part becoming the property of its own and original property turns into a new object, often abstract, in relation to an original object. Finally, it is worth noting that prospective atomicity of any property depends on a domain-oriented point of view.

Theorem (conceptual object simplicity): Let P_O be a set of all properties of an object O, and, s be a subset of it, and, c be a concept, and, finally, predicate cm denotes a conceptual meaning of its argument. We assert that the following is true:

$$\forall s \subset P_O \rightarrow \neg \exists c = cm(s) \tag{7}$$

Alternatively say, there is no conceptual meaning of any subset of object properties, i.e., all object properties are simple concepts in relation to it. If we need to work with a group of object properties as if it was one concept in itself, the group becoming an object of its own, with its own properties, often abstract, related to an original object. Again, it is worth noting that prospective conceptualisation of any subset of properties depends on the domain-oriented point of view.

A simple explanation of the above-introduced theorems with the aid of an example relating to the name of a person is demonstrated in the sequel. So, if we work in the domain of our special-interest always with the full personal name as a single concept encompassing both first and last personal name, we can comprehend this property as atomic and unique in view of the concept of person.

However, if we need to work, in the domain of our special-interest, with the first and last name separately, then the personal name becomes an abstract concept by itself with two properties (the first name property and the last name property). On the contrary, if the concept of person has two properties, a first and last name, and we need to work with this pair of properties any time jointly, the pair becomes a single concept by itself with its own denomination, in others words, the pair is a new named concept.

In the end, it is important not to overlook the fact that in the conceptual world it is necessary to think of a conceptual meaning of properties always in the context of just at that moment used the domain-oriented point of view.

3.3 The Base for Conceptual Normalisation

Firstly, we must remind that our approach of conceptual normalisation arises from primary presumption about a non-redundancy of Real World, and all the Author's subsequent considerations used in this article arise from the basic assumption formally articulated as follows:

> ***Axiom (about non-redundancy):*** *There is no redundancy in Real World.*   (8)

Let us appreciate the following facts. All objects in the real world exist only in one occurrence. Each human being is a unique individual, and there is only one occurrence of the SOFSEM 2012 conference etc. In other words, in Real World, there are not any two identical instances of the same object existing at the same time and space. Information systems hold a model of Real World by means of included data, so it is clear that as Real World exists without any redundancy, thus the model of that Real World also has no any redundancy.

It is worth noting that it is not the case of warehouses that use redundancy to achieve certain specific features. Similarly, database practises frequently rise above the mentioned principles to achieve an increasing throughput in the database system.

3.4 Definition of Redundancy

We can informally define redundancy as the non-existence of identical objects (concepts) in the system and can be formally defined as follows:

Definition (redundant system): Let S be a system, and, x, y be concepts of it, and, cm be a predicate denoting the conceptual meaning of its argument. We define a predicate RS denoting redundant system formally as:

$$RS(S) \stackrel{\text{def}}{=} \Box \exists x, y \in S, cm(x) = cm(y) \tag{9}$$

Definition (non-redundant system): Let S be a system, and, x, y be concepts of it, and, cm be a predicate denoting the conceptual meaning of its argument. We define a predicate NRS denoting non-redundant system formally as:

$$NRS(S) \stackrel{\text{def}}{=} \Box \forall x, y \in S, cm(x) \mathrel{!=} cm(y) \tag{10}$$

In other words, we can say that a redundant system contains at least two concepts with the same conceptual meaning, and, conversely, a non-redundant system has no concepts with the same meaning.

It is assumed that the Real World is a non-redundant system; therefore, all mappings of them to any information system result in a non-redundant system as well. Simply put, the mapping must be isomorphic in the domain of our concern.

Finally, it is worth noting that there are different types of redundancy of the system, concerning the level of system or instance scheme. However, in detail analysis of these issues falls outside the scope of this work.

4   Results: Proposals of Conceptual Normal Forms (CNFs)

In the previous section, we have formally defined the concepts of redundancy and non-redundancy of the system. Therefore, we may propose the definitions of conceptual normal forms which are understood as the rules of redundancy prohibition already introduced above and here altogether mentioned again in the sequel. We start this section with the group of informal definitions directly based on previously submitted assertions.

0CNF: *There is no redundancy in the real world.*
1CNF: *A set of object properties is unique in relation to it.*
2CNF: *An object property is not dividable; in other words, the object property is atomic. If we need to work with its part, this part becomes the object of its own, often abstract, with its own properties.*
3CNF: *If we need to work with a group of object properties as if it was one concept in itself, the group becomes the object of its own, often abstract, with its own properties.*

For now, we can formally define these informal definitions as follows:

Definition (0CNF): Let *WR* be *Real World* and, x, y be concepts of it, and, predicate *cm* denotes s conceptual meaning of its argument. We define *0CNF* formally as:

$$0CNF(WR) \overset{\text{def}}{=} \Box \forall x, y \in S, cm(x) \mathrel{!}= cm(y) \tag{11}$$

Definition (1CNF): Let *WR* be *Real World*, and, O be an object from it, and, the predicate *in* denotes a set of all properties of that object, and, predicate *cm* denotes a conceptual meaning of these properties. We define *1CNF* formally as:

$$1CNF(WR) \overset{\text{def}}{=} \Box \ \forall O \in WR, \forall p, q \in in(O), cm(p) \mathrel{!}= cm(q) \tag{12}$$

Definition (2CNF): Let *WR* be *Real World*, and, O be an object from it, and, P_O be a set of all properties of an object O, and, p be a property of that set, and, c be a concept, and, finally, predicate *cm* denotes a conceptual meaning of its argument. We define *2CNF* formally as:

$$2CNF(WR) \overset{\text{def}}{=} \Box \forall O \in WR, \forall p \in P_{0,} \ \neg \exists c \sqsubseteq cm(p) \tag{13}$$

Definition (3CNF): Let *WR* be *Real World*, and, O be an object from it, and, P_O be a set of all properties of an object O, and, s be a subset of it, and, c be a concept, and, finally, predicate *cm* denotes a conceptual meaning of its argument. We define a *3CNF* formally as:

$$3CNF(WR) \overset{\text{def}}{=} \Box \forall O \in WR, \forall s \subset P_{0,} \ \neg \exists c = cm(s) \tag{14}$$

The grounds for these conceptual normal forms have been introduced previously. The Authors believe that the relational and object forms can be derived from these more common conceptual forms. This can be briefly described in the following section.

4.1 CNFs in Relation to Relational Normal Forms (RNFs)

The Author of this article suggests that 1RNF arises from herein proposed 0CNF to 2CNF. The basis for this suggestion comes from the fact that 1RNF deals with atomicity of data attributes, the prohibition of multi-attributes and the necessity of primary key existence. Evidently, the issue of atomicity relates to the herein proposed 2CNF, the prohibition of multi-attributes results from 1CNF and the issue of the necessity of the primary key existence relates to principal 0CNF.

Further, the Author suggests that 2RNF is a specialisation, by specific manner, of more common 3RNF, but a more detailed discussion of this issue is outside the parameters of this article. This means that both 2RNF and 3RNF follow from above-suggested 3CNF. The evidence is based on the consideration that transitive dependency between relational keys at the level of the relational data paradigm is simply an implication of the incorrect recognition of conceptual objects at a higher level of comprehensibility.

Finally, it is worth noting, that the concept of relational keys in relational database systems by itself presents only the programmer implementation of the concept of functional dependency by the implication of mutual relationships among conceptual objects. Thus, the incorrect recognition of objects at the conceptual level leads to a transitive dependency between relational keys in the relational level. The all above mentioned connections between all types of normal forms are intelligibly depicted in Fig. 2.

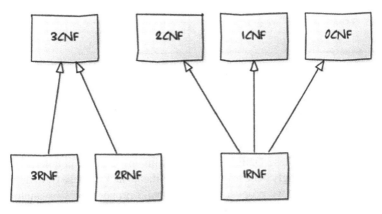

Fig. 2. Connectedness between CNFs and RNFs

4.2 CNFs in Relation to Object Normal Forms (ONFs)

Some authors emphasise a right designed object-oriented model of the information system, for instance [27, 28], among others. The BORM methodology [29] as example emphasises normalised object model as well. Currently, there is not any standard or commonly accepted concept of object normal forms.

Notwithstanding, there are many scientists engaged in this issue. A brief survey of these very different concepts is included in Molhanec and Merunka [20]. Moreover, this work contains definitions of object normal forms based on an approach introduced originally by Codd in [8] and further elaborated by them. Even though these authors deal with the object-oriented paradigm, the definitions of object normal forms are mostly based on analogical relational forms, i.e., 1ONF is based on 1RNF, and so on. This analogy is not entirely rigorously because the 2RNF has not a direct counterpart.

Furthermore, the fundamental difference of these ONFs definitions in comparison with definitions of RNFs lies in fact, that these are constructed without the use of relational keys concept naturally. The all ONFs mentioned above by Molhanec and Merunka and its connections with our CNFs are intelligibly depicted in Fig. 3.

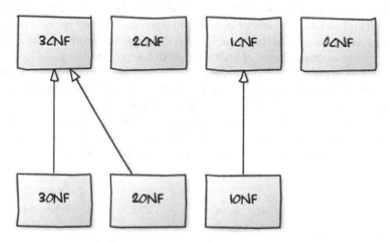

Fig. 3. Connections between ONFs and RNFs

To summarise this section, we can say that these definitions of ONFs are indeed very similar to the definitions of CNFs proposed herein with respect the exceptions before mentioned and we can apply the same or very similar argumentation for their reasoning. However, it is clear that these ONFs do not deal with any analogy counterparts of our 0CNF and 2CNF. We strongly believe that it is a significant lack of these ONF definitions.

Therefore, in the end, we propose an idea to build proper ONFs by analogy with CNFs proposed herein. However, it is clear that we have to proper reformulate all that conceptual definitions with the aid of object-oriented paradigm terms.

5   Conclusion and Future Works

In this paper, the Author deals with the issue of conceptual normalisation but also proposes the definitions of conceptual normal forms. The formalisation is based on intensional sortal modal logics (i.e., intensional modal logics with quantification restricted by sortal) with minimum additions to it.

Although this paper presents mainly the theory of conceptual normal forms, it can immediately bring practical benefits. Classical relational normalisation deals primarily with database keys and their values. However, we are primarily concerned with the meaning of classes, objects and properties in the conceptual plane. This approach allows us to think about the whole problem at a higher level of abstraction. This allows us to understand the issue better and thus create the right model. The result may be a correct relational model since we start from a higher abstraction of reality from the beginning.

The same is correct for object normalisation, where object normalisation theory is not yet completed and is not even considered necessary. At other times, it simply mimics relational normalisation. Even in this case, knowledge of conceptual normalisation leads to proper object normalisation and thus to the correct object model.

Further, the Author also suggests that relational and object normalisations jointly arise from the same source, i.e., from the conceptual normalisation. Surprisingly, this principal and serious subject matter are not widely discussed in the expert community at all. Also, the need for object normalisation that directly arises from the conceptual one is often disputed.

Moreover, it is worth noting that this proposal is only a part of the extensive author's work in this area. The insinuated way of a possible creation of object normal forms will be developed and argued in the future work of the Author. Firstly, there is a goal to build proper ONFs by analogy with CNFs proposed herein. Secondly, we aim to define formal methods of derivation RNFs and ONFs from CNFs. Eventually; we develop a universal ontology-based theory of normalisation generally.

Finally, the Author believes that his contribution in this exciting and serious subject matter can be a good starting point for the discussion of this issue in the frame of international expert community engaging in conceptual, object and data modelling.

References

1. Molhanec, M.: A contribution to user interface modelling based on graph transformations approach. In: Proceedings of the International Workshop on Enterprises & Organizational Modeling and Simulation, p. 14 (2009)
2. Molhanec, M.: Towards the conceptual normalisation. In: Proceedings of the 6th International Workshop on Enterprise & Organizational Modeling and Simulation, pp. 133–141 (2010)
3. Molhanec, M.: Conceptual normalisation formalised. In: Barjis, J., Eldabi, T., Gupta, A. (eds.) EOMAS 2011. LNBIP, vol. 88, pp. 159–172. Springer, Heidelberg (2011). https://doi.org/10.1007/978-3-642-24175-8_12
4. Molhanec, M.: Some reasoning behind conceptual normalisation. In: Pokorny, J., Repa, V., Richta, K., Wojtkowski, W., Linger, H., Barry, C., Lang, M. (eds.) Information Systems Development, pp. 517–525. Springer, New York (2011). https://doi.org/10.1007/978-1-4419-9790-6_41
5. Molhanec, M.: Úvod do konceptuální normalizace. In: Tvorba softvare 2010, Ostrava, pp. 141–149 (2010)
6. Molhanec, M.: Krátká úvaha o normalizaci. In: Objekty 2009, Hradec Králové, pp. 149–160 (2009)
7. Molhanec, M.: Ontologické základy konceptuální normalizace. In: Objekty 2006, Ostrava, pp. 81–90 (2006)
8. Codd, E.F.: A relational model of data for large shared data banks. Commun. ACM **13**(6), 377–387 (1970)
9. Codd, E.F.: Further normalization of the data base relational model. Data Base Syst. 33–64 (1972)

10. Codd, E.F.: Recent investigations into relational data base systems, IBM Research Report RJ1385, 23rd April 1974
11. Chen, P.P.-S.: The entity-relationship model—toward a unified view of data. ACM Trans. Database Syst. TODS **1**(1), 9–36 (1976)
12. Benci, E., Bodart, F., Bogaert, H., Cabanes, A.: Concepts for the design of a conceptual schema. In: IFIP Working Conference on Modelling in Data Base Management Systems, pp. 181–200 (1976)
13. Halpin, T.A.: What is an elementary fact? In: Proceedings of First NIAM-ISDM Conference (1993)
14. Pícka, M., Pergl, R.: Gradual Modeling of Information System
15. Ambler, S.W.: Building Object Applications that Work. Cambridge University Press, New York (1997)
16. Nootenboom, H.J.: Nuts - an online column about software design
17. Yonghui, W.: Research on normalization design for complex object schemes. In: 2001 International Conferences on Info-Tech and Info-Net. Proceedings (Cat. No. 01EX479), vol. 3, pp. 355–360 (2001)
18. Tari, Z., Stokes, J., Spaccapietra, S.: Object normal forms and dependency constraints for object-oriented schemata. ACM Trans. Database Syst. TODS **22**(4), 513–569 (1997)
19. Khodorkovsky, V.V.: On normalization of relations in databases. Program. Comput. Softw. **28**(1), 41–52 (2002)
20. Molhanec, M., Merunka, V.: Object normalization as the contribution to the area of formal methods of object-oriented database design. In: Sobh, T. (ed.) Advances in Computer and Information Sciences and Engineering, pp. 100–104. Springer, Dordrecht (2007). https://doi.org/10.1007/978-1-4020-8741-7_55
21. de Carvalho, V.A., Almeida, J.P.A., Guizzardi, G.: Using reference domain ontologies to define the real-world semantics of domain-specific languages. In: Jarke, M., Mylopoulos, J., Quix, C., Rolland, C., Manolopoulos, Y., Mouratidis, H., Horkoff, J. (eds.) CAiSE 2014. LNCS, vol. 8484, pp. 488–502. Springer, Cham (2014). https://doi.org/10.1007/978-3-319-07881-6_33
22. van Orman Quine, W.: Ontological Relativity and Other Essays. Columbia University Press, New York (1969)
23. Guizzardi, G.: Ontological foundations for structural conceptual models (2005)
24. Heller, B., Herre, H.: Ontological categories in GOL. Axiomathes **14**(1), 57–76 (2004)
25. Guizzardi, G., Wagner, G., Guarino, N., van Sinderen, M.: An ontologically well-founded profile for UML conceptual models. In: Persson, A., Stirna, J. (eds.) CAiSE 2004. LNCS, vol. 3084, pp. 112–126. Springer, Heidelberg (2004). https://doi.org/10.1007/978-3-540-25975-6_10
26. Guizzardi, G., Wagner, G.: Some applications of a unified foundational ontology in business modeling. In: Business Systems Analysis with Ontologies, pp. 345–367. IGI Global (2005)
27. Knott, R., Merunka, V., Polak, J.: The BORM methodology: a third-generation fully object-oriented methodology. Knowl. Based Syst. **16**(2), 77–89 (2003)
28. The Elements of UML™ Style (Sigs Reference Library): Scott W. Ambler: 9780521525473: Amazon.com: Books. https://www.amazon.com/Elements-UML%C2%99-Style-Reference-Library/dp/0521525470. Accessed 23 May 2019
29. Knott, R.P., Merunka, V., Polak, J.: The BORM methodology: a third-generation fully object-oriented methodology. Knowl. Based Syst. **16**, 77–89 (2003)

Object-Oriented Class Normalisation
from a Conceptual Modelling Perspective

Vojtěch Merunka[1,2(✉)], Himesha Wijekoon[1], and Boris Shegolev[1]

[1] Department of Information Engineering, Faculty of Economics and Management,
Czech University of Life Sciences Prague, Prague, Czech Republic
`vojtech.merunka@fjfi.cvut.cz`, {`merunka,wijekoon,`
`shegolev`}`@pef.czu.cz`
[2] Department of Software Engineering, Faculty of Nuclear Sciences and Engineering,
Czech Technical University in Prague, Prague, Czech Republic

Abstract. This article deals with an original view on the Ambler's approach to the object-oriented class normalisation from the perspective of conceptual modelling. This idea gives the possibility of using the object-oriented class normalisation rules not only for the design of composition structure of classes but also for the inheritance and inheritance-like structure of classes. This article also proposes a new systemisation of the object-oriented class normalisation and suggests further research. The authors applied their practical experience not only in teaching object-oriented programming at a university but also many years of experience in software development, especially in Smalltalk, C++, Java and C#.

Keywords: Object-oriented class normalisation · Conceptual modelling · Inheritance · Mixins · Symmetry

1 Introduction

Software engineers and practitioners are often confronted with the question "How to design the best structure of classes?" In the past, by the enthusiasm of the benefits of object-oriented programming, it was widespread that the object-oriented computation model automatically supports the right design, so programmers don't need much of formal techniques. At that time, the only widely used design technique was following set of requirements analysis rules: From the textual description of requirements, select verbs and you have methods, select nouns, and you have objects, select adjectives, and you have attributes... [2]. Later it was found that this is not enough and there were invented various object-oriented modelling techniques similar to the design of a relational database normalisation, decomposition or synthesis. Unfortunately, these techniques are still neither standard nor widely known and used today.

In this paper, we bring our own improvement to the widely used Ambler's approach [1] to the class normalisation. Our approach extends the original method by adding to two modelling levels - data and metadata. This leads to interesting new conclusions and also unification with current trends in the field of conceptual modelling.

© Springer Nature Switzerland AG 2019
R. Pergl et al. (Eds.): EOMAS 2019, LNBIP 366, pp. 29–39, 2019.
https://doi.org/10.1007/978-3-030-35646-0_3

2 Motivation

Software engineering community knows a few different approaches for the object-oriented class normalisation, but one can find some common ground. The first three object-oriented normal forms are more or less similar in most cases. Significant differences occur only in higher object-oriented normal forms, if they are defined at all. Finding a unifying view of this issue would certainly be of great benefit.

Next, in the physical world, the *symmetry* is an observable mathematical feature of a real system that remains unchanged under some transformation. There is also the *analogy* which is an effect of mapping some structure of one subsystem to another structure of another subsystem. Symmetries and analogies are maybe the most essential principles of how God is building the world and deserves our special attention. For example, the Russian chemist Dmitri Mendeleev did the same when he published the first widely recognised periodic table of chemical elements in 1869. He developed his periodic table to illustrate repeating properties of the then-known elements, and he also predicted some properties of then-unknown elements that would be expected to fill gaps in this table. Most of his predictions were proven correct when the new chemical elements were subsequently discovered. Analogically, we expected similar effect if the object-oriented normalisation rules were systematised in a similar way.

3 Current Approaches to the Object-Oriented Class Normalisation

Relational database normalisation has been introduced to reduce data redundancy and improve data integrity in relational databases via a concept called normal forms which initially ranged from first to three normal forms (1NF, 2NF, 3NF) [3, 4]. Later it is extended until sixth normal form (6NF). Each normal form deals with some steps to enhance the design to minimise anomalies based on reducing functional dependencies among attributes of relations.

Researchers have been interested on normalisation of object-oriented structures from early 1990s [12]. Initially these researches were emphasised on improving relational techniques to be effectively used in object-oriented systems as in [14], for example. With the advent of object-oriented databases, the focus has also moved towards object-oriented class normalisation. Object-oriented database normalisation was introduced as class normalisation by Ambler [1]. Hence notable initial ideas regarding object-oriented normalisation has been proposed by Ambler. His approach is discussed in detail in Sect. 4.

Lohdi and Mehdi have attempted to map the relational database normalisation concepts for object-oriented design [11]. But they have skipped 1NF mentioning it limits storage of complex objects. Apart from that, they have covered 2NF, 3NF, 4NF and 5NF. The get and set methods are also taken into consideration when applying the normalisation rules similar to attributes.

In a very recent paper Lo et al. have come up with seven steps for object-oriented normalisation [10]. Their approach was based on both Ambler's class normalisation and relational database normalisation concepts. They have taken Ambler's approach until the third object-oriented normal form (3OONF) and have come up with 4OONF similarly to the 4th relational database normal form. But in contrast to Ambler's steps, they suggest generalisation to eliminate homogenous operations between classes.

There have been also few researches to normalise object-oriented design not analogically to relational database normalisation. Falleri et al. have proposed a methodology to remove duplicate attributes by introducing general classes [5]. Their approach is based on Relational Concept Analysis (RCA) and supports Model Driven Engineering (MDE) by automating discovery of new classes and attributes when normalising. Ubaid et al. have come up with Class Hierarchy Normal Form Pattern (CHNFP) to maintain class schema in an object-oriented database [15]. CHNFP helps to manage objects and their network of objects in a memory efficient manner by optimising the object graph loaded into the memory by controlling the inheritance hierarchy.

4 Ambler's Approach to the Object-Oriented Class Normalisation

S. W. Ambler is a pioneer of agile approach in programming. He has published three object-oriented normal forms for object-oriented applications [1]. These normal forms are similar to the first, second and third relational normal forms but use a different theoretical apparatus than relational normal forms. The relational normalisation is based on the functional dependencies between separate attributes but Ambler's rules are based on various relationships of different subsets of attributes. Ambler talks also about these object-oriented normal forms as a tool for class structure design complementary with the technique of design patterns. Let's look at his approach in terms of our formalisation.

First Object-Oriented Normal Form - Multivalues

Rule 1. *A class is in the first object-oriented normal form (1OONF) when its objects do not contain group of repetitive attributes. Repetitive attributes must be extracted into objects of a new class. The group of repetitive attributes is then replaced by the link to the collection of the new objects. An object schema is in the 1OONF when all of its classes are in the 1OONF.*

Definition 1. Let us have an object a, where for $k \geq 1$ (length of collections of repeating attributes) and $n > 1$ (number of repetitions of these repeating collections) is $data(a) = \left[\ldots, x_1^1, \ldots, x_1^k, \ldots, x_n^1, \ldots, x_n^k, \ldots\right]$, having $\forall i \in (1, \ldots, k): domain\left(x_1^i\right) = domain\left(x_2^i\right) = \ldots = domain\left(x_n^i\right)$. Then it is required to modify the object a and create a collection of new objects $\{b_j\}$ for $j \in (1, \ldots, n)$ as $data(a) = \left[\ldots, \{b_j\}, \ldots\right]$ and $data\left(b_j\right) = \left[x_j^1, \ldots, x_j^k\right]$.

There is our example model of an object-oriented implementation of some *air travelling* information system which registers *e-tickets* in Fig. 1. This is a well-known document for most travellers because today most of them buy tickets on the Internet and then go to the airport with this *e-ticket* (printed on a piece of paper or only visible on a handheld screen) and personal documents and luggage. A typical *e-ticket* includes at least two *flights*: from home airport to destination and then back home. If there are connection *flights*, it is normal that *e-ticket* includes yet more individual *flights*.

Figure 1 presents the situation before normalisation basically similar as it appears printed on paper, for example. Figure 2 shows the same model transformed by our rules into the first object-oriented normal form. This example model is only a little simplified compared to reality. Practically, *e-tickets* have yet a few more detailed attributes that we don't need here for a demonstration of our approach to the object-oriented class normalisation.

```
┌─────────────────────────────────────────────┐
│             Electronic Ticket               │
├─────────────────────────────────────────────┤
│ +booking ref                                │
│ +issue date                                 │
│ +ticket nr                                  │
│ +traveller name                             │
│ +traveller category                         │
│ +traveller passport nr                      │
│ +traveller phone                            │
│ +traveller e-mail                           │
│ +total fare                                 │
│ +agency name                                │
│ +agency phone                               │
│ +agency e-mail                              │
│ +1st flight nr                              │
│ +1st flight class                           │
│ +1st flight seat nr                         │
│ +1st flight meal                            │
│ +1st flight operator name                   │
│ +1st flight equipment name                  │
│ +1st flight departure airport name          │
│ +1st flight departure datetime              │
│ +1st flight arrival airport name            │
│ +1st flight arrival datetime                │
│ +2nd flight nr                              │
│ ...                                         │
│ +3rd flight nr                              │
│ ...                                         │
│ +nth flight nr                              │
│ ...                                         │
└─────────────────────────────────────────────┘
```

Fig. 1. Air traveling example – Electronic Ticket in the non-normalised form.

Second Object-Oriented Normal Form – Shared Values

Rule 2. *A class is in the second object-oriented normal form (2OONF) when it is in the 1OONF and when its objects do not contain an attribute or a group of attributes, which is shared with another object. Shared attributes must be extracted into new objects of a new class, and in all objects, where they appeared, must be replaced by the link to the object of the new class. An object schema is in the 2OONF when all of its classes are in the 2OONF.*

Definition 2. Let us have two objects a, b for $k \geq 1$ (length of a collection of shared attributes) as $data(a) = [\ldots, x_1, \ldots, x_k, \ldots]$ and $data(b) = [\ldots, y_1, \ldots, y_k, \ldots]$ having $\forall i \in (1, \ldots, k)$: $x_i \equiv y_i$. Then it is required to modify objects a, b and to create new object c as $data(c) = [x_1, \ldots, x_k] = [y_1, \ldots, y_k]$ and $data(a) = [\ldots, c, \ldots]$ and $data(b) = [\ldots, c, \ldots]$.

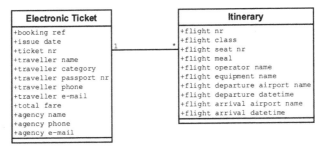

Fig. 2. Air traveling example – Electronic Ticket in the 1st object-oriented normal form.

In our example, the shared data are on individual *flights* as well as the *agency* that sold the *e-ticket*. There are hundreds of passenger places on one plane, so every person has their own *seat* and *flight class* and yet maybe *meal* (e.g. an *Itinerary* object), but the *flight* info is the same for all passengers. Similarly, the info about the selling company is the same on all *e-tickets* issued by the same company. That is why we have created two new classes *Agency* and *Flight* as shown in Fig. 3.

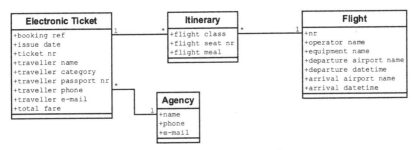

Fig. 3. Air traveling example – Electronic Ticket in the 2nd object-oriented normal form.

Third Object-Oriented Normal Form – Independent Values

Rule 3. *A class is in the third object-oriented normal form (3OONF) when it is in the 2OONF and when its objects do not contain an attribute or a group of attributes, which has an independent interpretation in the modelled system. The independent attributes must be extracted into object of a new class and in objects, where they originally appeared, must be replaced by the link to this new object. An object schema is in the 3OONF when all of its classes are in the 3OONF.*

Definition 3. Let us have an object a for $k \geq 1$ (length of a collection of independent attributes) having $data(a) = [\ldots, x_1, \ldots, x_k, \ldots]$, where $[x_1, \ldots, x_k]$ is a collection of independent attributes. Then it is required to create a new object b and modify the object a as $data(a) = [\ldots, b, \ldots]$ and $data(b) = [x_1, \ldots, x_k]$.

In our example, four other classes have become extracted following this 3OONF rule: *Traveller*, *Operator*, *Equipment*, and *Airport*.

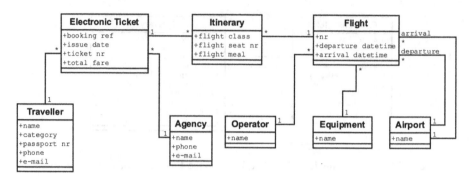

Fig. 4. Air traveling example – Electronic Ticket in the 3rd object-oriented normal form.

5   Class Inheritance

Of course, *composing* object classes is a significant building element for the object-oriented approach, but equally important is class *inheritance*. Although the presence of inheritance between object classes is not a prerequisite for an object-oriented model of calculation, because there exist object-oriented systems without classes or without inheritance, but class-based object-oriented systems with the inheritance constitute a de-facto standard. It is, therefore, striking that the development of formal class design techniques does not address the inheritance sufficiently.

Mixins

In object-oriented programming languages, a *mixin* is a structure similar to a class that contains methods for use by other classes without having to be the parent class of those other classes. *Mixins* are *traits* (e.g. sets of independent methods that can be used to extend the functionality of objects) which are used to compose classes. *Mixins* usage is sometimes described as being "included" rather than "inherited". At the conceptual level, it can be said that *mixins* are technical tools for better software implementation of the *decorator* design pattern [9].

Perhaps it can be said yet differently: some design patterns are made to solve the tasks for which programming languages has no direct support:

- If a programming language supports *mixins*, there is no need to use the *decorator* design pattern.
- Similarly, if a programming language supports *migration* instances between classes, there is no need to use the *state* design pattern, as it is in the Gemstone/Smalltalk programming language [7].

6   Our Proposal for Extension of Object-Oriented Class Normalisation

Our basic idea is as follows: Existing three rules for object-oriented normal forms relate to the properties of attribute data values and result in the *composing structure* (or *has-a hierarchy*) of classes. We could use the same three rules once more but on the level of attribute data types (e.g. one meta-level higher) and obtain the result in the *inheritance or inheritance-like structures* (or *is-a hierarchy*) of classes. By doing this we can get three more object-oriented normal forms which are presented in Table 1.

Table 1. Normal forms on the data and metadata levels.

data types level attribute data types INHERITANCE	4OONF ? .	5OONF sharing behaviour in subclasses	6OONF independent behav- iour in mixins
data values level attribute data values COMPOSING	1OONF multivalues within objects	2OONF sharing values within objects	3OONF independent values within objects

Fifth (Made from the Second) Object-Oriented Normal Form – Shared Data Types

Here it is enough to use definition from the 2OONF and only replace all occurrences of the term *value* with *type* and *object* by *class*. Let's look at the result:

Rule 4. *A class is in the fifth object-oriented normal form (5OONF) when it is in the 4OONF and when its objects do not contain an attribute or a group of attributes, whose attribute types are shared with another object. Shared attribute types must be extracted into new class linked as an inheritance superclass of all classes of objects, where they originally appeared. An object schema is in the 5OONF when all of its classes are in the 5OONF.*

Definition 4. Let us have two classes a, b for $k \geq 1$ (length of a collection of shared attribute types) as $datatypes(a) = [\ldots, x_1, \ldots, x_k, \ldots]$ and $datatypes(b) = [\ldots, y_1, \ldots, y_k, \ldots]$ having $\forall i \in (1, \ldots, k)$: $x_i \equiv y_i$. Then it is required to modify classes a, b and to create new class c as $datatypes(c) = [x_1, \ldots, x_k] = [y_1, \ldots, y_k]$ and $superclass(a) = c$ and $superclass(b) = c$ (otherwise $c \prec a$ and $c \prec b$).

In our example from Fig. 4, we have the opportunity to share the attribute type *name* in five classes: *Traveller, Agency, Operator, Equipment*, and *Airport*. But it would be foolish to create them all one common ancestor because they do not share exactly the same conceptual thing. The same technical implementation of their *name* attribute (as *String* or *Varchar*) does not mean that it is the same conceptual data type because, for example, *Traveller* names (e.g. human names) form a completely different set from the set of *Equipment* names (which includes, for example, Airbus A320, Boeing 737, ATR 72 …). The same is valid for names of *airports*.

Therefore, it makes sense to build inheritance and give a common superclass ancestor to only two subclasses *Agency* and *Operator*, as shown in Fig. 5.

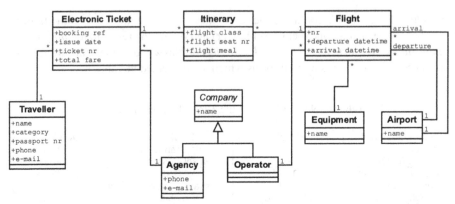

Fig. 5. Air traveling example – Electronic Ticket in the 5th (made from the 2nd) object-oriented normal form.

Sixth (Made from the Third) Object-Oriented Normal Form – Independent Data Types

Here it is also enough to use definition from the 3OONF and only replace all occurrences of the term *value* with *type* and *object* by *class*. Let's look at the result:

Rule 5. *A class is in the sixth object-oriented normal form (6OONF) when it is in the 5OONF and when do not contain an attribute type or a group of attribute types, which has an independent interpretation in the modelled system. These attribute types must be extracted into a new mixin and in classes where they originally appeared, must be replaced by the link to this new mixin. An object schema is in the 6OONF when all of its classes are in the 6OONF.*

Definition 5. Let us have a class a for $k \geq 1$ (length of a collection of independent attribute types) having $datatypes(a) = [\ldots, x_1, \ldots, x_k, \ldots]$, where $[x_1, \ldots, x_k]$ is a collection of independent attribute types. Then it is required to create a new *mixin* b as $datatypes(b) = [x_1, \ldots, x_k]$ and add *mixin* b to the class a.

In our example, such a transformation can be done for classes *Traveller* and *Agency*. Both classes use attributes *phone number* and *e-mail*. Of course, in cases where our programming language does not support *mixins*, we would need to use the *Decorator* design pattern [6]. The result is shown in Fig. 6.

7 Discussion

We presented that Ambler's rules for the 2OONF and 3OONF can be applied not only to the data values of attributes but also one meta-level higher, that is, to the data types of attributes. At the first level, these rules design the structure of class compositions (e.g. *has-a* relationships), and on the second level, principally the same rules design the structure of inheritance and inheritance-like (e.g. *is-a* relationships).

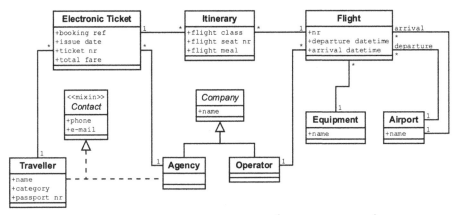

Fig. 6. Air traveling example – Electronic Ticket in the 6th (made from the 3rd) object-oriented normal form.

The empty box in Table 1 in the 1OONF on the type level remains an unanswered question. There might be an interesting solution; the first normal form is so specific that its definition directly covers both levels. Such a solution is shown in Table 2. However, it would disrupt the symmetry in our table. Of course, the periodical table of Mendeleev is also not absolutely symmetrical, but it has clear evidence from practice. In our case, only the idea about the hypothesis of analogy cannot be enough to prove us.

Table 2. Normal forms on the data and metadata levels – an alternative solution

data types level attribute data types INHERITANCE	1OONF	4OONF sharing behaviour in subclasses	5OONF independent behav- iour in mixins
data values level attribute data values COMPOSING	multivalues within objects	2OONF sharing values within objects	3OONF independent values within objects

The evolution of the object-oriented paradigm has always been guided by spontaneous evolution from practice. Perhaps an interesting solution lies in the dual physical implementation of object classes in some programming languages. They are ordinary classes with a fixed number of uniquely named instance variables, and so-called variable classes, where the number of instance variables is variable. An example of such a language is Smalltalk-80 [8].

In our example, there is seen yet one interesting feature of Ambler's rules for object-oriented normalisation of classes. Figure 3 shows that the class *Agency* and the class *Flight* were separated by the 2OONF rule because more objects of the class *Electronic Ticket* have shared the same data about *Agencies* and *Flights*. However, these two classes *Agency* and *Flight* can also be separated with the same result under the 3OONF rule if we had not used the 2OONF rule before. This is why *Agency* data and *Flight* data are also independent on issued *Electronic Tickets*.

Therefore, we can conclude that 2OONF and 3OONF are closely related and perhaps could represent two special cases of only one rule. This phenomenon of Ambler's 2OONF and 3OONF was also described in [13]. However, in our experience for good practical reasons, it is not appropriate to simplify these two rules into one rule only because there exist some real situations when both rules are applicable to the same structure and produce the same result. Even though in these situations, it does not really matter whether we separated a new class according to the 2OONF rule or the 3OONF rule, the existence of two rules still gives us greater certainty of better result.

8 Conclusion

This paper has presented an innovative approach to the object-oriented class normalisation technique. This approach enables the generalisation and the explanation of some connections with other object-oriented design pattern techniques and advanced inheritance-related constructs of modern programming languages which are *mixins* and *traits*. Based on our own experience, we believe that our proposal allows members of the development team to improve the quality of their software engineering work, reduce uncertainty and improve conceptual consistency.

We think that the major theoretical contribution of this paper is an alternative perspective on the current object-oriented design techniques, which provides a solid foundation for both future theoretical research and also its practical implementation in some CASE tools that support automated or semi-automated class structure modelling, for example in our experimental tool *OpenPonk* [16]. In detail:

1. We added *inheritance* to the object-oriented normalisation rules.
2. We showed new conceptual connections (analogy, symmetry) between the object composing and the object inheritance.
3. We found a theoretical reason of inheritance-like programming constructs *trait* and *mixin*.
4. We have confirmed the previously known idea that behavioural design patterns can be replaced by direct semantic constructs in some programming languages. Either our language allows *mixins* or we need to use a *decorator* design pattern, but at the conceptual level, it is the same.
5. Perhaps we have found a place for yet one more new inheritance-like conceptual modelling property. This remains an unsolved question for the future.

Our future research will focus on the empirical justification of our statements and programming algorithms of conceptual model transformation according to our rules of the object-oriented normal forms.

References

1. Ambler, S.W.: Agile Database Techniques: Effective Strategies for the Agile Software Developer. Wiley Publishing, Inc., New York (2003). ISBN 978-0-471-20283-7

2. Coad, P., Yourdon, E.: Object-Oriented Design. Yourdon Press and Prentice Hall, Inc., Englewood Cliffs (1991). ISBN 0-13-630070-7
3. Codd, E.: A relational model of data for large shared data banks. CACM **13**(6), 377–387 (1970)
4. Codd, E., Rustin, R.: Further Normalisation of the Database Relational Model in Database Systems. Prentice Hall, Englewood Cliffs (1972)
5. Falleri, J.-R., Huchard, M., Nebut, C.: A generic approach for class model normalisation. In: Proceedings of the 2008 23rd IEEE/ACM International Conference on Automated Software Engineering (ASE 2008), Washington, DC, USA, pp. 431–434. IEEE Computer Society (2008). https://doi.org/10.1109/ASE.2008.66
6. Gamma, E., Helm, R., Johnson, R., Vlissides, J.: Design Patterns: Elements of Reusable Object-Oriented Software with a Foreword of Grady BOOCH. Addison-Wesley Professional, Reading (1995). ISBN 978-0201633610
7. Gemstone: GemStone/S v6.7.1 Programming Guide, GemStone Systems, Inc. (2018)
8. Goldberg, A., Robson, D.: Smalltalk-80: The Language and Its Implementation. Addison-Wesley Professional, Reading (1989). ISBN 978-0201136883
9. Hollemans, M.: Mixins and Traits in Swift 2.0 (2015). http://machinethink.net/blog/mixins-and-traits-in-swift-2.0/
10. Lo, S.-H., Shiue, Y.-C., Liu, K.F.: Seven steps for object-oriented normalisation in class diagrams: example of jigsaw puzzle concept for image retrieval. J. Appl. Sci. Eng. **21**, 463–474 (2018). https://doi.org/10.6180/jase.201809_21(3).0018
11. Lodhi, F., Mehdi, H.: Normalisation of object-oriented design. In: 7th International Multi Topic Conference, INMIC 2003, Islamabad, pp. 446–450 (2003). https://doi.org/10.1109/INMIC.2003.1416768
12. Mok, W.Y., Ng, Y.K., Embley, D.W.: An improved nested normal form for use in object-oriented software systems. In: Proceedings of the 2nd International Computer Science Conference: Data and Knowledge Engineering: Theory and Applications, Hong Kong, pp. 446–452 (1992)
13. Molhanec, M.: Conceptual normalisation formalised. In: Barjis, J., Eldabi, T., Gupta, A. (eds.) EOMAS 2011. LNBIP, vol. 88, pp. 159–172. Springer, Heidelberg (2011). https://doi.org/10.1007/978-3-642-24175-8_12
14. Naiburg, E.J., Maksimchuk, R.A.: UML for database design. In: Chapter 7 - Database Design Models - The UML Profile for Database Design. Addison Wesley Longman, Inc., Reading (2003). ISBN 0201721635
15. Ubaid, M., Atique, N., Begum, S.: A pattern for the effective use of object-oriented databases. In: 2009 International Conference on Information and Communication Technologies, Karachi, pp. 229–234 (2009). https://doi.org/10.1109/ICICT.2009.5267187
16. Uhnak, P., Pergl, R.: The OpenPonk modelling platform. In: Proceedings of the 11th Edition of the International Workshop on Smalltalk Technologies, pp. 14:1–14:11 (2016). https://doi.org/10.1145/2991041.2991055

Enterprise Engineering

Evolvable and Machine-Actionable Modular Reports for Service-Oriented Architecture

Marek Suchánek[✉] and Jan Slifka

Faculty of Information Technology, Czech Technical University in Prague,
Prague 6 16000, Czech Republic
{marek.suchanek,jan.slifka}@fit.cvut.cz

Abstract. Independent and preferably atomic services sending messages to each other are a significant approach of Separations of Concerns principle application. There are already standardised formats and protocols that enable easy implementation. In this paper, we go deeper and introduce evolvable and machine-actionable reports that can be sent between services. It is not just a way of encoding reports and composing them together; it allows linking semantics using technologies from semantic web and ontology engineering, mainly JSON-LD and Schema.org. We demonstrate our design on the Data Stewardship Wizard project where reports from evaluations are crucial functionality, but thanks to its versatility and extensibility, it can be used in any message-oriented software system or subsystem.

Keywords: Service-Oriented Architecture · Reports · Messaging · Machine-actionability · Evolvability

1 Introduction

Complex software systems of these days are usually composed of integrated parts to achieve better flexibility, re-usability, and separation of concerns [3]. Service-oriented architecture (SOA) and so-called microservices are one of the often-used means for designing such systems allowing integration with external third-party services [9]. Many protocols, formats, techniques, such as SOAP, Messaging Queues, REST, or Enterprise Service Buses, already exist to support this approach in software engineering, but we still encounter missing parts on the higher level of implementation – the content of messages.

When there is an integration need where one part (i.e. a client) should request an action from some other component (i.e. a service), the response is usually a message with a service-specific format, and it is up to the client to implement the mechanism to accept the message [3]. As for the syntactic level, there are libraries and frameworks for standard formats, but on the semantic level, it gets more complicated. Standard protocols provide none or minimal semantics (e.g. return codes) to remain versatile. Due to that, the client needs to implement its own

© Springer Nature Switzerland AG 2019
R. Pergl et al. (Eds.): EOMAS 2019, LNBIP 366, pp. 43–59, 2019.
https://doi.org/10.1007/978-3-030-35646-0_4

way of "understanding" for each integration since no semantic standardisation is provided to enable machine-actionability and re-usable libraries.

For machine-actionable data and semantic networks, RDF is often used together with ontological RDF schema or even using the Web Ontology Language (OWL) to describe the types, relations, and properties. One of the great examples is the Schema.org for the semantic web, which also uses JSON-LD for encoding Linked Data using traditional and widely-used JSON format [13]. Those technologies could be used to design modular architecture for reports sent by services in SOA that would be easily evolvable in terms of creating and changing types of reports or enriching its content and also that would be machine-actionable and yet versatile.

Initially, we briefly introduce the terminology and summarise state-of-the-art and related work in Sect. 2 that is then used to design our solution. In Sect. 3, we describe the requirements, architecture and general usage of our evolvable and machine-actionable modular reports. Then, we demonstrate it on the specific use case. We explain the semantics as well as the syntax of our solution. Section 4 evaluates our contribution and its critical properties based on the design and demonstration; it also summarises fulfilment of the set requirements. Finally, Sect. 5 we propose possible directions for further research and practical usage.

2   Related Work

This section briefly describes state-of-the-art and related work in the area of our work and also provides the necessary terminological and theoretical background for the following design of evolvable reports for SOA.

2.1   SOA and Microservices

Service-oriented architecture (SOA) as described in [3] is a style of building software that is based on services which are known using contract (i.e. they are black-box) and are provided to others via communication protocols. The main idea is that each service has its task as suggested in the *Separation of Concerns* principle and they communicate using some messages in a defined and documented way. There are multiple approaches on how to implement SOA, such as web services based on WSDL and SOAP, messaging, or RESTful APIs. With SOA, there is also the term *Microservices* that goes even further. Microservices are fine-grained, and the protocols are lightweight implementing a single functionality and using other services for other tasks conforming *low coupling* and *high cohesion* [9].

2.2   Messaging in SOA

Message-based integration is crucial in nowadays complex software systems and many tools, frameworks, and design patterns have been developed to support and enhance it. One of the fundamental integrator types is an enterprise service bus (ESB). It can be described as a communication system between mutually interacting SOA applications using various protocols and interfaces. Part of ESB but also stand-alone can be so-called message broker that is a component that can be used for message validation, transformation, enrichment, routing and more. It often uses a message queue (MQ) that allows gathering messages for further processing and in most cases supports publisher/subscriber pattern [1]. Our solution will be designed universally to be used with such tools and patterns.

2.3 Machine-Actionability

When we talk about *machine-actionable* reports, we use the definition by Data Documentation Initiative [2] which described machine-actionable documents as "information that is structured consistently so that machines, or computers, can be programmed against the structure". It says that the structure of a document is well-designed and computers can process it efficiently. On the other hand, no speculations or assumptions how the machines will handle it and what specific actions will be done (i.e. autonomous communication or transformations). There is a clear analogy to widely-known term *human-readability* that is similar, just that the document is structured and composed with intention to simplify reading by human beings.

The term *machine-actionable* is mainly emphasised lately in the domain of data management plans and metadata [12,18]. Reasons for both cases are very straightforward. For metadata, tools need to be able to process them to effectively work with data that are being described and to provide help to scientists or data analysts. In the case of data management plans, funders, project supervisors, or other stakeholders need to quickly evaluate how data are or should be managed in the selected projects. If the structure is well-defined and standardised, i.e. documents or metadata are machine-actionable, then these tasks are relatively easy to do.

2.4 RDF and OWL

Resource Description Framework (RDF) enables knowledge modelling and capturing using descriptions of generic terms in a graph. It uses intensively Uniform Resource Identifiers (URIs) for linking inside and outside the single document. The core unit of knowledge in RDF is a single triplet consisting of a subject, a predicate, and an object which is universal and is both machine-actionable and human-readable using both graphical visualisations or textual representations. The structure, i.e., a set of possible relationships and a vocabulary, in RDF can be described using RDF Schema (RDFS) or more precisely using the Web Ontology Language (OWL). These technologies are currently used for the semantic web, open data, bioinformatics, and many others and are well supported by libraries, frameworks, and persistence solutions in various programming languages [7].

2.5   JSON-LD

JavaScript Object Notation for Linked Data [13] is a W3C recommendation of encoding Linked Data using JSON which is widely used in the semantic web. The core of linking in JSON-LD is about mappings of JSON with RDF models using a context that connects concepts in an ontology with object properties in a JSON document. The format allows modularity and reusability in terms of the context definition inside single JSON-LD file or a separate reusable file. It can be easily written and read by a human but thanks to vast of libraries for JSON and extensions for JSON-LD it can be easily machine-actionable as well.

JSON-LD has already been used for adding semantics and assuring evolvability in RESTful web services [5]. The syntax, which is compatible with JSON, allows smooth upgrade of existing tools and services.

There are implementations of JSON-LD available in a variety of programming languages, such as Java, C# or JavaScript [17]. We can assume that the format will be used in the future because new tools and libraries are still arising, e.g., for TypeScript and NodeJS [14].

2.6   Schema.org

Schema.org [4] is a community project to develop a vocabulary for semantic web that is usable via many formats including JSON-LD, RDFa and Microdata (i.e. annotated HTML with special attributes `itemscope`, `itemtype`, and `itemprop`). The schemas of Schema.org are *types* defined with their properties, and property can use some of the defined types. There are basic data types such as `Text` or `Boolean` but also more complex types like `Person` or `SoftwareApplication`, each with its unique canonical URL. There are *layers* and standard versioning to allow easy extensibility for different domain schemas, so anyone can build their extension if needed. As it is a community project, discussions and contributions can be done via GitHub [11].

2.7   Normalized Systems Theory

Normalized Systems (NS) theory [6] is general guideline based on solid mathematical proofs how to build an evolvable system with a fine-grained modular structure. It clarifies design concepts from software engineering fields, such as separation of concerns or data version transparency, and specifies how to use them in practical use cases among various areas – not just software engineering. Nevertheless, software engineering is a domain where Normalized Systems have a significant impact using NS expanders that allow creating from a specification an enterprise information system that conforms with NS theory [10]. We acknowledge NS theory as the primary source of knowledge for building evolvable and modular systems as are reports described in this paper, and we apply the core principles. It is described then in Sect. 4 how the evolvability with respect to NS is achieved.

2.8   Data Stewardship Wizard

A tremendous amount of data is produced during research in biology, chemistry, artificial intelligence, and others. Researchers of those fields are not experts in information technologies and data management. In order to assure correct work with data (e.g. data will be stored with rich metadata for a long period of time in a universal repository using standard formats and protocols), data management plans (DMPs) are often required for project funding [8]. To help researchers build DMPs and learn how to work with their data in projects, the Data Stewardship Wizard provides a way how to construct elaborate questionnaires using so-called knowledge models. The questionnaire can be linked to various types of integrations to help researchers with answering or interlink external services and resources. Answers can then serve to generate a DMP using a specific template to various formats [15].

We want to use the results of research in this paper to enrich the Wizard with flexible and extensible Evaluators. The core idea is that an answered questionnaire can be evaluated in many ways, and reports from evaluators can be different in their structure and meaning. For example, some evaluator can calculate values for specific metrics and return scores, others can give textual feedback, and a certification evaluator can return certificate ID or denial. Of course, we do not want to implement a specific format for each, but universal and extensible one for straightforward future development.

3   Our Approach

This section describes what the reports in the Data Stewardship Wizard are, our requirements, where we started from, how we transformed our original report format into a new one that is evolvable, modular and machine-actionable. Then, we show an example of how clients can use the new format.

3.1   Reports

The workflow for researchers in the Data Stewardship Wizard starts with selecting a knowledge model (which is a template for hierarchical questionnaire) that suits the needs of the research project. Then, the Wizard guides researchers through the relevant chapters and questions of the questionnaire. Once the questionnaire is filled, researches can export the data management plan. They can also evaluate the plan using so-called evaluators.

An evaluator is a service that reads the answers from the questionnaire and evaluates some of its properties. For example, the result of the evaluation could be expected costs for data storage or compliance with the FAIR principles [18]. The result of the evaluation, which we call **report**, should contain the data presented in a machine-actionable way so that other services can process it.

If we use a standard format which is easily readable by machines, we can simplify the complexity of implementation of services consuming the reports, thus reduce the development costs.

3.2   General Requirements

The reports should be used not only within the Data Stewardship Wizard but also in other tools which we do not know about yet. Therefore, it is essential to provide them in a format that can be easily read by other computer programs and services. Moreover, we need to achieve some level of modularity because the number of different reports is not fixed and we will have new types in the future. We want to have a relatively small amount of components we can compose together to create the final report. These components should be reusable in different reports so that the clients can implement those and support new reports out of the box.

We already used the JSON format in our API for communication between our client and backend. JSON itself does not say anything about the meaning of the data within though. It might be clear for the original authors but not for the third parties. The documentation is somewhere else (if anywhere), so the developers, that want to consume the reports, have to be aware of it and implement a custom reading mechanism to understand the data in their intended application. That is not very modular nor evolvable and requires much work when new types and changes in existing types of reports are released.

We need a format that

- is easy to read by machines,
- contains not only the data itself but also metadata,
- allows creating our metadata,
- supports modularity.

3.3   Selected Technologies for Implementation

Even though JSON itself does not contain the metadata, it is still a prevalent format used in a vast amount of nowadays APIs. As a consequence, there are plenty of tools and libraries for using JSON. The ideal solution for this situation seemed to be JSON-LD (JSON for Linking Data) format, which is based on JSON. It provides a way to include metadata and links to other entities within the JSON document itself.

Moreover, JSON-LD has available libraries for popular programming languages (like Python or Java), making it easier for third parties to use our reports. They have significant advantages over the already mentioned pure-JSON libraries that are also possible to be used thanks to identical syntax. It often helps with querying linked data and doing validations over JSON-LD specific parts.

The JSON-LD format works in a way that the document contains links to the definitions to describe the structure and the meaning of the data. We can use Schema.org for common entities. In our case, however, we have a lot of particular entities that are not available in Schema.org. The good thing is, we can define our schema for the Data Stewardship Wizard where we describe new entities, link their properties to existing entities in Schema.org and make the new schema publicly available. As long as the consumers can understand the meaning of the entities from Schema.org, they can derive the meaning of our entities as well.

3.4   Original Report Format

Our original report format was a plain JSON. You can see an example of FAIRness report in Source Code 1.1. It contains several report fields – a summary text, values for different metrics and final score and result of the evaluation. It worked fine as long as we used it between our client and server. However, it is evident that reading and understanding the JSON for a third party would be hard, almost impossible without proper documentation. This format is also not very modular. Our goal is to be able to compose different reports from small reusable pieces. Now we have a fixed structure for each type of report.

Source Code 1.1: Original report JSON structure

```
 1  {
 2      "uuid": "<uuid>",
 3      "title": "FAIR Metrics Report",
 4      "createdAt": "2019-03-04T10:46:18.193223736Z",
 5      "updatedAt": "2019-03-04T10:46:18.193223736Z",
 6      "report": {
 7          "text": "...",
 8          "metrics": [{
 9              "measure": 0.75,
10              "metricUuid": "<uuid>"
11          }, {
12              "measure": 0.8,
13              "metricUuid": "<uuid>"
14          }],
15          "score": {
16              "value": 0.87,
17              "passed": true
18          }
19      }
20  }
```

3.5   Modularity and Reusability of Reports

Before moving further, we need to resolve the modularity. The top-level object representing report looks all right. We should model the fields in the report section in a different way though. We can replace report object with a list of different types of report modules. Later we can combine those modules to form new reports. Example of how we transformed score into a report module is shown in Source Code 1.2.

Source Code 1.2: ScoreReportModule structure

```
1  {
2     "type": "ScoreReportModule",
3     "value": 0.87,
4     "passed": true
5  }
```

Then, we need to slightly modify the top level structure of the report by replacing the *report* object with *reports* array (Source Code 1.3).

Source Code 1.3: Report JSON structure with improved modularity (report modules skipped for brevity)

```
1  {
2      "uuid": "bad6f3c5-7f86-456a-9979-c418972bad89",
3      "title": "FAIR Metrics Report",
4      "createdAt": "2019-03-04T10:46:18.193223736Z",
5      "updatedAt": "2019-03-04T10:46:18.193223736Z",
6      "reports": [
7
8      ]
9  }
```

We can handle the modularity this way. When we need a new report module in the future, we can add it and combine it with existing ones to form new reports. Introducing a report module that would reuse other report modules as its parts is also possible and in some cases might be very useful in terms of reusability and composability. The readers of the report format would not have to implement a whole new report structure but only the new report module.

Speaking of readers of reports, we still have a problem with the understanding of what the keys and values in the report mean. That makes reusability and machine-readability of them in different applications hard. Luckily, we can significantly improve that using JSON-LD. The order of reports in the list should not matter and be up to the client application to prioritise them based on type or source. The important thing is that a service producing a report can aggregate multiple reports into one, and the same type of report module can be repeated.

3.6   Transformation of Report Schema

First of all, we should define the entities which the report consist of. We have UUID, title, and timestamp of creation and update. Then we have several report modules. Text module which is just a text that should be visible when showing the report. Metrics module which contains a list of measures (values between 0 and 1) and UUIDs for each metric. In the end, we have a scoring module with a final result.

We can say a report consists of its identifier, name, timestamps, and a list of report modules. For now, we have a text module, metrics module, and score module. For the sake of completeness and consistency, we decided to expand metrics in the metric report to include their name and description. The new structure is shown in Fig. 1.

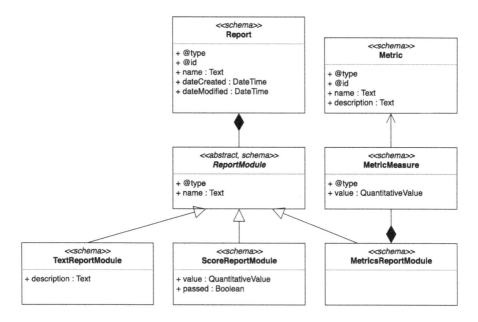

Fig. 1. Schema of the report model

We needed to rename some fields to define their meaning clearly. Instead of using our field names, we used existing fields and types from Schema.org.

We also changed all the values in our report to use *QuantitativeValue* type from Schema.org that includes the upper and the lower bounds, which can be useful when displaying the report. Till now, we know what the range was and hardcoded it into the client that was displaying the report. The information should be, however, included in the report.

Since not everything we required was available in Schema.org, we had to define our own fields and types. The following tables shows the schema for Report (Table 1), ReportModule (Table 2), TextReportModule (Table 3), MetricMeasureModule (Table 4, ScoreReportModule (Table 5), MetricMeasure (Table 6) and Metric (Table 7). The fields and types from Schema.org are prefixed with *schema* and our new fields and types are prefixed with *dsw*.

Table 1. Report schema fields

Field	Expected type	Description
schema:name	schema:Text	A name of the report
schema:dateCreated	schema:DateTime	Date and time when the report was created
schema:dateModified	schema:DateTime	Date and time when the report was modified
dsw:reportModules	dsw:ReportModule	List of report modules

Table 2. ReportModule schema fields

Field	Expected type	Description
schema:name	schema:Text	A name of the report module

Table 3. TextReportModule schema

Field	Expected type	Description
schema:description	schema:Text	A text description that is part of the report
+ fields from ReportModule		

Table 4. MetricMeasureModule schema

Field	Expected type	Description
dsw:metricMeasures	dsw:MetricMeasure	A list of values for different metrics
+ fields from ReportModule		

Table 5. ScoreReportModule schema

Field	Expected type	Description
schema:value	schema:QuantitativeValue	Score value
dsw:passed	schema:Boolean	Represents whether the result of report was successful
+ fields from ReportModule		

Table 6. MetricMeasure schema

Field	Expected type	Description
schema:value	schema:QuantitativeValue	The result value for the metric
dsw:metric	dsw:Metric	A metric that was evaluated

Table 7. Metric schema

Field	Expected Type	Description
schema:name	schema:Text	A name of the metric
schema:description	schema:Text	A description of the metric

3.7 The New Report

Following the process described in previous chapters, we transformed the original plain JSON report (mentioned in Source Code 1.1) into a JSON-LD format that contains all the necessary metadata Source Code 1.4.

3.8 Workflow of Reports Processing

Let us say we updated our client to support the new modular structure that we defined before moving to JSON-LD (Source Code 1.3). However, we have different keys in our JSON now due to the transformation to JSON-LD. Do we need to update our client again? Luckily no, JSON-LD is not only useful for enriching the data with metadata and meaning. If we provide a new context, it can remap all the fields from the original context to the new one.

For example, when we apply a context from Source Code 1.5 to our new report format from Source Code 1.4 we get a result shown in Source Code 1.6. It is still a valid JSON-LD. However, the keys in the document are the same as in the report before we started using JSON-LD. So with this easy transformation, we can use it with our original client code.

This example shows how easy it is to remap the fields to a new context with JSON-LD. Should the report be used in a different application, it is possible to follow the same steps to transform it into a format that can be easily readable by the target application.

4 Evaluation

In this section, we briefly summarise the fulfilment of the requirements and key properties of the designed evolvable reports in terms of usability and extensibility.

Source Code 1.4: The new report structure

```
1   {
2       "@context": {
3           "schema": "http://schema.org/",
4           "dsw": "http://schema.ds-wizard.org/"
5       },
6       "@id": "https://ds-wizard.org/reports/<uuid>",
7       "@type": "dsw:Report",
8       "schema:name": "FAIR Metrics Report",
9       "schema:dateCreated": "2019-03-04T10:46:18.193223736Z",
10      "schema:dateModified": "2019-03-04T10:46:18.193223736Z",
11      "dsw:reportModules": [{
12          "@type": "dsw:TextReportModule",
13          "schema:name": "Summary",
14          "schema:description": "..."
15      }, {
16          "@type": "dsw:MetricsReportModule",
17          "schema:name": "FAIR Metrics Result",
18          "dsw:metricMeasures": [{
19              "@type": "dsw:MetricMeasure",
20              "schema:value": {
21                  "@type": "schema:QuantitativeValue",
22                  "schema:maxValue": 1,
23                  "schema:minValue": 0,
24                  "schema:value": 0.75
25              },
26              "dsw:metric": {
27                  "@type": "dsw:Metric",
28                  "@id": "https://ds-wizard.org/metrics/<uuid>",
29                  "schema:name": "Fairness",
30                  "schema:description": "..."
31              }
32          }]
33      }, {
34          "@type": "dsw:ScoreReportModule",
35          "schema:name": "Total Score",
36          "schema:value": {
37              "@type": "schema:QuantitativeValue",
38              "schema:maxValue": 1,
39              "schema:minValue": 0,
40              "schema:value": 0.87
41          },
42          "dsw:passed": true
43      }]
44  }
```

Source Code 1.5: The new JSON-LD context

```
1   {
2       "@context": {
3           "schema": "http://schema.org/",
4           "dsw": "http://schema.ds-wizard.org/",
5           "title": "schema:name",
6           "createdAt": "schema:dateCreated",
7           "updatedAt": "schema:dateModified",
8           "reports": "dsw:reportModules"
9       }
10  }
```

Source Code 1.6: Report with a new context (report modules skipped for brevity)

```
1   {
2       "@context": {
3         "schema": "http://schema.org/",
4         "dsw": "http://schema.ds-wizard.org/",
5         "title": "schema:name",
6         "createdAt": "schema:dateCreated",
7         "updatedAt": "schema:dateModified",
8         "reports": "dsw:reportModules"
9       },
10      "@id": "https://ds-wizard.org/reports/<uuid>",
11      "@type": "dsw:Report",
12      "reports": [
13
14      ],
15      "createdAt": "2019-03-04T10:46:18.193223736Z",
16      "updatedAt": "2019-03-04T10:46:18.193223736Z",
17      "title": "FAIR Metrics Report"
18  }
```

4.1   Versatility

Our contribution in the form of evolvable reports architecture for service-oriented systems is not limited to any specific domain. It can be used in systems that communicate using messages of any type and any size. The advantages will have a higher impact with larger systems rather than systems composed of two nodes (e.g. for communication between server and client of a web application). Domain-specific requirements can be projected on the level of report modules that represent specific concerns. Aside from SOA, the format can be used even for storing reports and operations within a single application using, for instance, MongoDB and JSON-LD libraries.

4.2 Interoperability

High level of interoperability is achieved by using standard self-documented JSON-LD format. It is now effortless for other applications to integrate our reports into their functionality. Although the structure is not very complicated, it allows straightforward extensibility. The solution provides a required minimal structure in a report file, but services that are implementing our design in practice may freely add custom attributes and other constructs without losing compatibility with us.

The interpretation of a specific report type should be suggested by its developers, and the internal structure should be well described. When processing the report, the client freely decides based on @type attribute if and how it should be processed. Thanks to incorporating terms from Schema.org vocabularies, as well as the possibility to add others if needed, integration with other services is more accessible than if own terms are used. In such a case, the mapping would be required for the integration.

4.3 Machine-Actionability

As being back and forth translatable to/from RDF, JSON-LD format is by definition machine-actionable. It is even easier to implement the application for processing the report in this format thanks to defined attributes from standard ontologies and providing a mapping in the @context of a report. The semantics of the report modules should also be described in the same way, so the application knows the meaning of its parts again by using a linked ontology. These are critical advantages when compared to JSON, YAML, or even some custom formats.

4.4 Evolvability

We transformed our report structure to be composed of report modules. We can combine the modules differently and create new reports. When we need new modules, we can easily define them in our schema based on the publicly available ontology from Schema.org or elsewhere. Their meaning will be still obvious, and it should be easy to work with updated versions of the reports.

When developing new modules, we suggest to apply semantic versioning and backward compatibility, e.g., removed attributes should be just ignored, new attributes should have a default value for deprecated reports and so on. If such fundamental principles are maintained in modules, the whole report is evolvable. Owing to the independence of modules, there are no ripple effects, and the report modules can be processed in parallel and even if the processing of some fails, others might be used without a problem.

As we use Normalized Systems theory as a source of knowledge for developing an evolvable solution, the core principles can be discussed:

- Separation of Concerns: Each concern is encapsulated it a single report module. If a module should contain more concerns (e.g. textual description and related chart or dataset), then the report should also be composed of sub-modules.

– Data Version Transparency: Report modules are independent with each other and requirements on a module from a global perspective are minimal. Update of a structure inside a module is encapsulated without any impact "outside".
– Action Version Transparency: Action that process a single type of report module is again independent on others. Implementation of report processing can be composed of these simple actions, and they can be updated, again, without any impact on each other,
– Separation of States: This principle is more related to the implementation of chaining actions to process a report. The state of each action should exhibit state keeping, and there are no obstacles given by our report structure.

5   Future Work

The solution designed in this work is entirely usable but still can be further improved, extended, and used in specific use cases where more research might be needed, and new exciting results can emerge. We briefly describe a few next steps that we want to work on in the near future.

5.1   Application in Data Stewardship Wizard

The first impulse for this research was the need for universal and extensible reports from integrations to the DSW, and the goal remains to implement it and use widely for evaluations of questionnaires and data management plans. We plan to build integrations using Apache Camel [16] where our reports will be generated from an output of external services and then it will be passed through server application on client's request. There are multiple challenges in our vision. First, integration modules will use the same report's model but will be independent on each other and on the server application itself. Then, the server will also be independent and should pass the requests and responses between integrations and the client application transparently. Finally, the client will implement its way of displaying various types of report modules and reuse them for multiple evaluations.

5.2   Enhancements with Specialized Modules

Naturally, as we described in this paper, more types of report modules can be designed and used within our architecture without any changed thanks to ensured evolvability. Aside from pure application-specific modules, there can be domain-specific modules described and used within multiple applications. For that, we could introduce a unified way of sharing such descriptions and enhance our work with them. We might encounter interesting obstacles in that when modules will need to have submodules or if more complex content such as binary data, encrypted content for higher security, and incorporating asynchronous communication in the architecture. It can lead to further research to design evolvable solutions for such significant changes.

5.3 Support for Programming Languages

Designing the format and architecture of the reports is just the first step. Implementations in real use cases are necessary to prove its principles by practice and actually to help. To ensure implementation according to our visions and to support its usage in practice, libraries and tools for programming languages should be developed. Apparently, such libraries will be done as side-product of incorporating the reports in our projects in languages we use, such as Haskell, Elm, and Java. Nevertheless, thanks to its architecture and overall simplicity, it should not be too hard to implement it for other main-stream languages used in SOA, e.g., Python, Ruby, and Node.js.

6 Conclusion

In this paper, we designed architecture, processing, and structure of evolvable and machine-actionable reports that can be used in service-oriented software systems. Our contribution is focused on further extensibility for specific use cases. Thanks to selected technologies, mainly the usage of JSON-LD format and terms from Schema.org vocabulary, we achieved evolvability, interoperability, and machine-actionability. The report modules are up to the specific applications to be developed and described as we have shown a few simple but real and not trivial examples. We pursue a goal to use the results of this research for Data Stewardship Wizards to implement independent evaluators with common high-level reports structure and processing.

Acknowledgements. This research was supported by the grant of Czech Technical University in Prague No. SGS17/211/OHK3/3T/18. The work on the Data Stewardship Wizard is partially funded by IOCB of the CAS and ELIXIR infrastructure.

References

1. Chappell, D.: Enterprise Service Bus. O'Reilly Media, Inc., Newton (2004)
2. DDI Alliance: Machine-actionable (definition) (2018). https://www.ddialliance.org/taxonomy/term/198. Accessed 21 May 2019
3. Erl, T.: Service-Oriented Architecture: Analysis and Design for Services and Microservices. Prentice Hall Press, New Jersey (2016)
4. Guha, R.V., Brickley, D., Macbeth, S.: Schema.org: evolution of structured data on the web. Commun. ACM **59**(2), 44–51 (2016). https://doi.org/10.1145/2844544
5. Lanthaler, M., Gütl, C.: On using JSON-LD to create evolvable RESTful services. Proceedings of the Third International Workshop on RESTful Design - WS-REST 12 (2012). https://doi.org/10.1145/2307819.2307827
6. Mannaert, H., Verelst, J., Bruyn, P.D.: Normalized Systems Theory: From Foundations for Evolvable Software Toward a General Theory for Evolvable Design. Koppa, Kermt (Belgie) (2016)
7. McGuinness, D.L., Van Harmelen, F., et al.: OWL web ontology language overview. W3C Recommendation **10**(10), 2004 (2004)

8. Mons, B.: Data Stewardship for Open Science: Implementing FAIR Principles. CRC Press, Boca Raton (2018). https://books.google.cz/books?id=-HhQDwAAQBAJ

9. Newman, S.: Building Microservices: Designing Fine-Grained Systems. O'Reilly Media Inc., Newton (2015)

10. Oorts, G., Huysmans, P., De Bruyn, P., Mannaert, H., Verelst, J., Oost, A.: Building evolvable software using normalized systems theory: a case study. In: 2014 47th Hawaii International Conference on System Sciences, pp. 4760–4769. IEEE (2014)

11. Patel-Schneider, P.F.: Analyzing schema.org. In: Mika, P., Tudorache, T., Bernstein, A., Welty, C., Knoblock, C., Vrandečić, D., Groth, P., Noy, N., Janowicz, K., Goble, C. (eds.) ISWC 2014. LNCS, vol. 8796, pp. 261–276. Springer, Cham (2014). https://doi.org/10.1007/978-3-319-11964-9_17

12. Simms, S., Jones, S., Mietchen, D., Miksa, T.: Machine-actionable Data Management Plans (maDMPs). Research Ideas and Outcomes 3 (2017). https://doi.org/10.3897/rio.3.e13086

13. Sporny, M., Longley, D., Kellogg, G., Lanthaler, M., Lindström, N.: JSON-LD 1.0. W3C Recommendation **16**, 41 (2014)

14. Sterling, A.: NodeJS and Angular Tools for JSON-LD. In: 2019 IEEE 13th International Conference on Semantic Computing (ICSC) (2019). https://doi.org/10.1109/icosc.2019.8665625

15. Suchánek, M., Pergl, R.: Data Stewardship Wizard for Open Science. Brno, Czech Republic (2018)

16. The Apache Software Foundation: Apache Camel. https://camel.apache.org. Accessed 23 May 2019

17. W3C: JSON for Linking Data. https://json-ld.org/. Acceesed 22 May 2019

18. Wilkinson, M.D., et al.: The FAIR guiding principles for scientific data management and stewardship. Sci. Data **3**, 160018 (2016)

Challenges in Enterprise and Information Systems Modeling in the Contexts of Socio Cyber Physical Systems

Marite Kirikova[✉] [iD]

Riga Technical University, 1 Kalku, Riga 1658, Latvia
marite.kirikova@rtu.lv

Abstract. Nowadays information systems extend beyond the traditional enterprise resource planning systems, which often are regarded as socio-technical systems. With availability of cloud computing, open data, smart devices and smart factories, information systems development requires considering enterprises as socio-cyber-physical systems with emerging relationships to other systems; and handling emerging data available in the cyberspace. Well known frameworks such as ArchiMate enterprise architecture language, Reference Architecture Model Industry 4.0, and Work System framework only partly can cover the needs of socio-cyber-physical systems modeling. There are several challenges in the application of these frameworks in information systems design in the contexts of socio-cyber-physical systems. To meet the identified challenges, some extensions and integration of the frameworks are suggested.

Keywords: Information system · Enterprise · Socio cyber physical system · ArchiMate · RAMI 4.0 · Work system framework

1 Introduction

Traditionally Enterprise Modeling (EM) and Information Systems (IS) are applied in the context of business organizations where, basically, the alignment of two types of systems is to be achieved. Namely, these systems are a business system and an IS. However, with the advances of artificial intelligence and new smart solutions, there are more alignments and more types of systems to be considered. Partly this issue can be covered by socio-technical systems approach. Socio-technical systems are often regarded as "complex systems where social (human and organizational) and technical components interact with each other to achieve common objectives" [1]. However, in many cases, these technical components are regarded just as a cyber space, i.e., software and hardware (including wireless networks). Physical devices with embedded cyber components and their interaction with other devices or human beings are rarely considered. Therefore, in this paper we will not take a position of socio-technical systems, but will rather consider social, cyber and physical systems and their interplay for embracing such concepts as Industry 4.0 (or cyber-physical systems - CPS), social networks and open data. We define a socio-cyber-physical system (SCPS) as a system that includes all three types of

© Springer Nature Switzerland AG 2019
R. Pergl et al. (Eds.): EOMAS 2019, LNBIP 366, pp. 60–69, 2019.
https://doi.org/10.1007/978-3-030-35646-0_5

elements: social, cyber and physical ones; and may include different combinations of these elements as subsystems).

The research approach taken in this paper is as follows. First the information system issues related to contemporary information usage variations is explored. Then these issues are related to and analyzed in the context of three enterprise and information systems modeling approaches/frameworks. The factors not covered by these approaches are identified as challenges in enterprise and information systems modeling.

The paper is organized according to the research approach taken. Section 2 concerns information system issues in the SCPS contexts. Section 3 ponders over possibilities to address these issues in several modeling frameworks, such as enterprise architecture representation language ArchiMate [2], Reference Architectural Model Industry 4.0 [3], and Work System model for defining information systems [4]. Section 4 discusses commonalities and differences of these frameworks and points to the related works in modeling of SCPSs. Section 5 presents brief conclusions and some directions of further research.

2   Information Systems in the Context of SCPS

Hirschheim and Klein [5] in 2012 referred to four eras in IS history:

- First era (mid 1960 – to mid 1970): Centralization
- Second era (mid 1970 – to mid 1980): User led IS development projects
- Third era (mid 1980 – mid 1990): Decentralization, emergence of Internet
- Fourth era (mid 1990 – today): Management of widely distributed technologies and personnel.

These four eras basically refer to an information system as "a manual or automated system, such as an automatic data processing system, a computer system, or a computer network, that (a) is composed of people, machines, or methods and (b) is organized to collect, process, transmit, and disseminate data that represent user information" [6]. Most often "machine" here is understood as computer software and hardware. Now in 2019, one of the most well-known conferences on IS, ICIS [7] calls for papers in such topics as Human Computer/ Robot Interactions & Interfaces; Analytics and Data Science; Crowds, Social Media and Digital Collaborations; Mobile, IoT and Ubiquitous Computing; Smart Cities and Digital Government; and Smart Service Systems and Service Science in line with the more traditional ones. This shows that an IS now shall concern physical devices, different emerging data sources, and *serve for systems of arbitrary combinations of such substances as social, cyber and physical systems*. Actually an IS itself often is a SCPS – "any configuration of a system that collects, organizes, stores, and distributes information" [6], where socio, cyber and physical (sub)systems can be receivers, handlers and providers of information.

In the context of SCPSs, an essential aspect of an IS is emergence (consider networks, open data, system collaboration, etc.), because not all issues regarding the IS can be under the control in CSPSs. In Table 1 we show a simple scheme of types of elements (or subsystems) of IS that are of different nature and can be included in an IS. In Table 1 only some examples of possible subsystems/elements are shown. The table demonstrates that in all cases we shall deal with both – the elements purposely developed and the elements that are emerging inside or outside the enterprise (a SCPS) under the consideration. Depending on the viewpoint, purposely developed elements of one enterprise can be emerging elements for another enterprise, e.g. purposely developed software services developed by Company A can emerge as new opportunities of Company B.

Table 1. Different types of subsystems or elements of IS (from an enterprise viewpoint)

Type of a subsystem or element	Developed in a controlled manner	Emerging
Social	Business process (manual); Rules of the game	Peer network
Cyber	Workflow engine, Database	World Wide Web
Physical	Factory equipment, sensor	Natural phenomena – such as weather conditions
Socio-cyber	Workflow	Social network, open data
Cyber-physical	Robot	Behavior of an intelligent multi-agent system (e.g. smart cars on the road)
Socio-physical	People acting according to a command	A human being interacting with a mechanical machine and natural object (e.g. stone)
Socio-cyber-physical	Passenger in a smart car (under the car's control)	Human being interacting with a robot

Similarly, and to some extent also consequently, taking into account the nature of the above-mentioned systems; also data sources and data used in information systems can be classified in the developed in a controlled manner (e.g. centralized databases, log data, etc.) and emerging ones (e.g. open data, information available in social networks, etc.). This issue impacts a possibility to define a border of an enterprise and a border of an information system. For instance, we can question whether a cloud service, which belongs to an information system, belongs also to an enterprise for which this information system serves.

Above mentioned IS issues are challenging the existing approaches of alignment of enterprises (SCPSs) and their information systems (see also discussion in Sect. 4).

In the next section we will analyze three well known frameworks regarding their appropriateness to handle enterprise controlled and emergent data and systems listed in Table 1.

3   Common Frameworks in the Context of SCPS

In this section we will analyze how several frameworks can be used to address the various IS issues (types of IS elements) explored in previous section. Three frameworks will be considered: enterprise architecture representation language ArchiMate [2], Reference Architectural Model Industry 4.0 [3], and Work System model for defining information systems [4]. These frameworks are chosen due to their popularity in the field of Information Systems Research.

3.1 Applicability of ArchiMate

ArchiMate is a well-known enterprise architecture representation language [4] that complies with the Open Group's managed enterprise architecture framework TOGAF [8]. The latest version of this language, which initially addressed only socio-cyber systems, includes new modeling elements for modeling physical systems. This new version of ArchiMate has already been analyzed with respect its applicability for cyber-physical systems [9], and some improvements have been suggested to address such issues as construct overload, redundancy, excess and deficit.

We will discuss here four layers of ArchiMate framework [4]: Business layer, Application layer, Technology layer, and Physical layer. Two other layers of the Archi-Mate framework, namely, Strategy and Implementation & Migration layers will not be discussed as they are out of the scope of the focus of this paper.

The Business, Application and Technology layers all have the same types of their passive structure (data belongs to passive structure elements), behavior (represents functions, processes, services, etc.) and active structure (elements which handle information or materials) elements. The Physical layer differs from these layers as it provides only "material" as a passive element and does not specify behavioral elements.

The representational capability of ArchiMate language layers regarding the systems listed in Table 1 is illustrated in Table 2.

Table 2. Representation capabilities of ArchiMate framework layers

ArchiMate layer	Represented system types
Business layer	Social, Physical (partly), Socio-Physical (partly)
Application layer	Cyber
Technology layer	Cyber Physical (partly), Physical
Physical layer	Physical (partly)

The Business layer of ArchiMate, from the point of view of socio-technical systems, would represent the social system ("business" might be considered as a social activity). However, in the context of SCPSs, a human being can be considered from two points of view – as an element of a social system and as an element of a physical system [10, 11]. The same refers also to passive elements of the Business layer (e.g. hard copies of documents also belong to physical systems). Elements of cyber systems are stretched over two layers (Application and Technology), where elements of the Technology layer can belong to both cyber and physical systems. It is not only because physical computing devices occupy a physical space; there can be cases where, e.g. heat generated by computers should be considered and then the role of computers changes from the data processing objects to the energy providing objects. As mentioned above, regarding the Physical layer, here such elements as "equipment", "facility", "distribution network" and "material" can be shown, however, the behavioral elements are missing at that level. This becomes challenging when robotic or other artificial multi-agent systems must be modeled.

ArchiMate language has no specific means to point to emerging systems or data, so it is basically appropriate for modeling of systems organized or built in a controlled manner. The language does not clearly distinguish in its layers among social, cyber and physical systems; therefore, it cannot transparently represent all these systems and their combinations. Also, the Physical layer has limited representational capability if compared to other layers discussed in Table 2. On the other hand, such elements as "path" and "communication networks" are available only at the Technology layer which does not allow abstracting from this layer at other layers.

In order to have more flexible abstraction possibilities and possibility to reflect artificial agent behavior at Physical layer, the following extensions to ArchiMate language would be welcome:

- Including "network" and "communication path" elements in all four layers (see Table 2).
- Providing at the Physical layer the same set of elements as at other three layers (Business, Application and Technology) of the ArchiMate framework.

3.2 Applicability of RAMI 4.0

While in the previous section we dealt with ArchiMate, which is a language for representation of a generic enterprise and has not been developed specifically for SCPSs, the wave of interest in cyber-physical systems has brought in several new models and frameworks [12], where The Reference Architecture Model Industry 4.0 (RAMI 4.0) is one of the most popular ones. RAMI 4.0 is a three-dimensional framework involving hierarchy levels, life cycle and value streams, and layers [13]. This framework is designed to serve smart factories. Enterprise is one of the hierarchy levels (one between Connected World and Work Centers). According to the framework, each hierarchy level (thus also the Enterprise) can be considered at 6 layers, namely Business, Functional, Information, Communication, Integration, and Asset layers.

Some researchers claim that RAMI4.0 provides some room for emerging systems and emerging data (through the connected world level of hierarchy and Communication and Integration layers) [10], however, they have not provided transparent models approving that claim. The framework is focused on cyber physical systems. It refers to human beings but does not consider social system issues in detail.

The system types concerned by layers of RAMI 4.0 at the Enterprise level are reflected in Table 3. More detailed description of RAMI 4.0 layers is available in [14]. This framework basically helps to represent how virtual world is related to the real world. It does not suggest specific modeling elements as ArchiMate language provides. The purpose of RAMI4.0 is not to transparently distinguish between social, cyber and physical systems; it rather is designed to control the physical systems with the help of cyber systems. Different modeling approaches for the use of this framework are still emerging [14–16].

Table 3. Representational capability of RAMI 4.0 layers (at the Enterprise level)

RAMI 4.0 layer	Represented system types
Business layer	Social (partly)
Functional layer	Cyber, Physical (partly)
Information layer	Cyber
Communication layer	Cyber, Physical (partly)
Integration layer	Cyber, Physical
Asset layer	Social, Physical

One of the directions of further studies could be an investigation of possibilities to apply extended ArchiMate language (see suggestions in the previous sub-section) to the RAMI 4.0 framework. This would be a complex task considering differences between RAMI 4.0 and TOGAF (to which ArchiMate has been adjusted). Nevertheless, ArchiMate has already established modeling tools and many modelers are skilled in this language due to its relative simplicity. With a possibility to clearly distinguish between systems of different types and their combinations, the ArchiMate language, probably, could be a suitable tool for reflecting different views of RAMI 4.0 SCPSs.

3.3 Applicability of Work Systems Framework

Work Systems is a flexible framework developed by American scientist Steven Alter [4]. The framework is theoretical and only first attempts to provide a supporting modeling method have been made [17]. The framework concerns Environment, Infrastructure and Strategies as a context in which particular activities or processes are done by Participants using Information and Technologies to produce Products or Services for Customers [18, 19]. This framework is attractive due to its simplicity. Obviously, it aligns with socio-technical systems perspective (Participants and Technologies) and do not directly distinguish between Social, Cyber and Physical Systems and heir combinations.

Nevertheless, a distinguished feature of the framework is the possibility to define work systems at different levels of detail and abstraction using the same generic frame. The approach has a potential to represent any combination of performers (be they parts of social, cyber or physical systems) as a work system performing activities or processes for providing products or services. The Work Systems framework can embrace elements form ArchiMate layers represented in Table 2 and RAMI 4.0 framework represented in Table 3. Therefore, it might be suitable as an umbrella frame for modeling socio-cyber-physical systems and their combinations. To achieve this, it is necessary to provide a modeling environment that helps to distinguish between different types of systems and their combinations, which means relating the elements under the consideration to all types of systems in which they participate, as each type of base systems is governed either by rules of social systems or computer code or physical laws.

4   Discussion

In Sect. 3, three well known frameworks were analyzed regarding their applicability for SCPS contexts of IS. Each framework exposed some capabilities and some limitations. These pros and cons are amalgamated in Table 4.

Table 4. Pros and cons of the frameworks analyzed in Sect. 3

Characteristic	ArchiMate	RAMI 4.0	Work Systems
1. Possibility to see transformations (input, function, output)	Yes	Yes	Yes
2. Modeling elements prescribed	Yes	No	In progress in related work [17]
3. Possibility to show all types of systems at the same level of detail	Partly	Yes[a]	Yes[a]
4. Possibility to distinguish clearly between all types of systems	No	No	No
5. Possibility to reflect (or distinguish) emerging systems	No	No evidence provided	No
6. Possibility to reflect emerging data	No	No	No

[a]Only on a high abstraction level

We can see that all frameworks provide general means for *representing transformations* done by systems; i.e. functions and their inputs and outputs can be shown in the frameworks; and also the performers of the functions. This is an essential feature to have a transparent systems perspective.

Only ArchiMate has its *modeling notation* (and also modeling tools) for representing the systems. RAMI4.0 does not prescribe any modeling language. Regarding Work Systems, there is some initial work done to relate it to a particular modeling notation [17]. Taking into account extensions suggested in Sect. 3.1, it might be useful to relate the frameworks so that ArchiMate notation could be used for representing the systems. It looks quite straight forward to relate ArchiMate to Work Systems framework. However there are conceptual differences regarding ArchiMate and RAMI4.0. These differences are reflected in Fig. 1. While both frameworks have layers, the meaning of these layers is different. Especially it concerns data. There is a separate layer for data in RAMI 4.0; and other layers are accessing this data. In ArchiMate, data is positioned at the Application layer, but data has references to business objects at the Business layer and artifacts at the Technology layer. Thus all layers are processing some kind of information. Similarly it is with functions. In ArchiMate, it depends on interpretation what exactly is regarded as physical assets: these could be people, devices and facilities each at their corresponding layers. In RAMI4.0, assets are at the dedicated Asset layer. Considering these differences, we can assume that relating RAMI4.0 and ArchiMate might require additional modeling elements to transfer the meaning of layers correctly from one modeling framework to another.

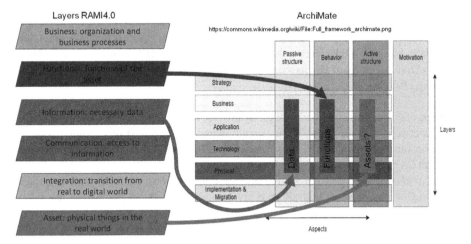

Fig. 1. Differences in layering of RAMI4.0 [3] and ArchiMate [2]

As was explained in Sect. 3.1, ArchiMate does not allow to model at the Physical layer in the same manner as at the Business, Application and Technology layers. Thus *all systems cannot be modeled equally*. Other two frameworks stay general with respect to particular modeling notations and are equally suitable for modeling social, cyber, and physical systems at the high level of abstraction. If suggested extensions would be implemented in ArchiMate, it could be suitable for equal representation opportunities for all three types of systems at a high level of abstraction and also in details.

None of frameworks give an opportunity to *clearly distinguish between different types of systems* (the fact that the system can be represented by the framework, does not yet say that it can be distinguished from other system types: e.g. computer at the Technology layer and Physical layer of ArchiMate, or Human being as an asset or as a participant of a the Business layer in RAMI4.0.

None of frameworks can clearly identify *emerging systems and emerging data.*

In this paper we concentrated on IS modeling in SCPS context. Some enterprise and IS aspects, in the context of SCPSs, have been discussed in a number of research papers. For instance, information and material flow models (on a high level of abstraction) are discussed in [20]; goal modeling integrated with systems modeling language SysML is proposed in [21], where the author uses only a goal model for representing social (sub)systems and SysML for cyber and physical sub(systems); and authors of [22] propose to integrate human factors in cyber physical systems by paying more attention to human-machine interaction and user interface design. None of these works provide models for representing transformation aspects in all three (social, cyber, physical) sub(systems). However, the findings from related works will be helpful in further research regarding modeling of socio-cyber-physical systems.

5 Conclusions

In this paper we discussed applicability of some well-known frameworks for modeling socio-cyber-physical systems: namely the enterprise architecture modeling language ArchiMate, Industry 4.0 Reference Architecture Model RAMI 4.0, and St. Alter's Work Systems framework were discussed. Brief analysis of these frameworks revealed the following challenges:

1. None of discussed frameworks currently provide means for transparently distinguishing between all types of systems (social, cyber, physical and their combinations). For instance, human being is positioned at the Business layer (ArchiMate) or at the Asset layer (RAMI 4.0).
2. To cover all three types of systems and their combinations, the ArchiMate language should be extended so that all core layers and the Physical layer have the same representational element types.
3. Regarding possibility to reflect all system types, RAMI 4.0 framework could benefit from its integration with extended ArchiMate language, however, to integrate them, the differences between TOGAF and RAMI 4.0 should be well understood.
4. Work System framework has a potential to be populated with the modeling tools for transparent modeling of social, cyber and physical systems and their combinations, but a mechanism must be found how to relate these systems to the rules by which the systems are governed.

This paper is limited to preliminary discussion on modeling socio-cyber-physical systems. Further research is needed to meet the above identified challenges and develop tools for transparent modeling of socio-cyber-physical systems from different perspectives or viewpoints. The necessity to model emerging systems and handle emerging data should also be considered in this context.

References

1. Salnitri, M., Paja, E., Giorgini, P.: Preserving compliance with security requirements in socio-technical systems. In: Cleary, F., Felici, M. (eds.) CSP 2014. CCIS, vol. 470, pp. 49–61. Springer, Cham (2014). https://doi.org/10.1007/978-3-319-12574-9_5
2. ArchiMate® 3.0.1 Specification, an Open Group Standard (2017). http://pubs.opengroup.org/architecture/archimate3-doc/. Accessed 17 Mar 2019
3. Schweichhart, K.: Reference Architectural Model Industrie 4.0 (RAMI 4.0). https://ec.europa.eu/futurium/en/system/files/ged/a2-schweichhart-reference_architectural_model_industrie_4.0_rami_4.0.pdf. Accessed 17 Mar 2019
4. Alter, St.: Defining Information systems as work systems: implication for the IS field. Bus. Anal. Inf. Syst. Paper 22 (2008). http://repository.usfca.edu/at/22. Accessed 17 Mar 2019

5. Hirschheim, R., Klein, H.K.: A glorious and not-so-short history of the information systems field. J. Assoc. Inf. Syst. **4**, 188–235 (2012)
6. Weik, M.H.: Information system. In: Weik, M.H. (ed.) Computer Science and Communications Dictionary. Springer, Boston (2000). https://doi.org/10.1007/1-4020-0613-6
7. International Conference on Information Systems ICIS 2019. https://icis2019.aisconferences.org/submissions/call-for-papers/. Accessed 17 Mar 2019
8. The TOGAF® Standard, Version 9.2 Overview. https://www.opengroup.org/togaf. Accessed 17 Mar 2019
9. Franck, T., Iacob, M.-E., van Sinderen, M., Wombacher, A.: Towards an integrated architecture model of smart manufacturing enterprises. In: Shishkov, B. (ed.) BMSD 2017. LNBIP, vol. 309, pp. 112–133. Springer, Cham (2018). https://doi.org/10.1007/978-3-319-78428-1_6
10. Stanescu, A.M., Repta, D., Moisescu, M.A., Sacala, I.S., Benea, M.: Towards a generic enterprise systems architecture based on cyber-physical systems principles. In: Camarinha-Matos, L.M., Afsarmanesh, H. (eds.) PRO-VE 2014. IFIPAICT, vol. 434, pp. 245–252. Springer, Heidelberg (2014). https://doi.org/10.1007/978-3-662-44745-1_24
11. Sandkuhl, K., Smirnov, A., Shilov, N.: Cyber-physical systems in an enterprise context: from enterprise model to system configuration. In: Abramowicz, W. (ed.) BIS 2015. LNBIP, vol. 228, pp. 148–159. Springer, Cham (2015). https://doi.org/10.1007/978-3-319-26762-3_14
12. Basl, J.: Analysis of Industry 4.0 readiness indexes and maturity models and proposal of the dimension for enterprise information systems. In: Tjoa, A.M., Raffai, M., Doucek, P., Novak, N.M. (eds.) CONFENIS 2018. LNBIP, vol. 327, pp. 57–68. Springer, Cham (2018). https://doi.org/10.1007/978-3-319-99040-8_5
13. Pisching, M.A., Pessoa, M.A.O., Junqueira, F., Miyagi P.: PFS/PN technique to model Industry 4.0 systems based on RAMI 4.0. In: 2018 IEEE 23rd International Conference on Emerging Technologies and Factory Automation (ETFA), vol. 1, pp. 1153–1156 (2018)
14. Mourtzis, D., Gargallis, A. Zogopoulos, V.: Modelling of Customer Oriented Applications in Product Lifecycle using RAMI 4.0. Procedia Manuf. **28**, 31–36 (2019). https://www.sciencedirect.com/science/article/pii/S2351978918313489. Accessed 31 Mar 2019
15. Pisching, M.A. Pessoa, M.A.O., Junqueira, F., Filho, D.J.S., Miyagi, P.A.: An architecture based on RAMI 4.0 to discover equipment to process operations required by products, Comput. Ind. Eng. **125**, 574–591 (2018)
16. Nardello, M., Møller, Ch., Gøtze, J.: Organizational learning supported by Reference Architecture Models: Industry 4.0 laboratory study. Complex Syst. Inform. Model. Q. CSIMQ, Issue (12), 22–38 (2017). https://doi.org/10.7250/csimq.2017-12.02. Accessed 31 Mar 2019
17. Alter, St., Bork, D.: Work System Modeling Method with Different Levels of Specificity and Rigor for Different Stakeholder Purposes (2019). http://eprints.cs.univie.ac.at/5841/. Accessed 31 Mar 2019
18. Alter, S.: The Work System Method: Connecting People, Processes, and IT for Business Results. Work System Press, Lankspur (2006)
19. Alter, S.: Work system theory: overview of core concepts, extensions, and challenges for the future. J. Assoc. Inf. Syst. **14**, 72–121 (2013)
20. Frazzon, E.M., Hartmann, J., Makuschewitz, T.H., Sholz-Reiter, B.: Towards socio-cyber-physical systems in production networks. Procedia CIPR **7**, 49–54 (2013)
21. Anda, A.A.: Modeling adaptive socio-cyber-physical systems with goals and SysML. In: Proceedings of IEEE 26th International Requirements Engineering Conference, pp. 442–447. IEEE (2018)
22. Stern, H., Becker, H.: Development of a model for the integration of human factors in cyber-physical production systems. Procedia Manuf. **9**, 151–158 (2017)

Proposing an Architecture of an Intelligent Evolvable Document Generation System Based on the Normalized Systems Theory

Vojtěch Knaisl[(⊠)]

Faculty of Information Technology, Czech Technical University in Prague,
Prague, Czech Republic
knaisvoj@fit.cvut.cz
https://ccmi.fit.cvut.cz

Abstract. In the current world, low evolvability of documents is a big challenge which has not been fully addressed. This paper focuses on types of documents which have mostly predefined structure, and we use them over and over. Examples of these documents are contracts, applications, legal documents or manuals. The key problem here is that the documents are not modular and evolvable. The problem of modularity and evolvability is addressed by Normalized Systems Theory. This theory is formally proven, and it has great practical results from the first application in a software area. This paper designs a way how to apply principles and recommendations from Normalized Systems Theory in the area of non-evolvable documents.

Keywords: Evolvable documents · Normalized Systems Theory · Document management · Modularity

1 Introduction

One of the main challenges of traditional documents is that they are non-evolvable. For many kinds of documents, it is not a problem. When we are creating a document for one-time usage, we do not have to care about evolvability. However, when we know that we will (re)use our document in future and we will need to edit it, update it or create a new one based on the structure of the first one, the non-evolvability of the traditional document may become a real problem.

Imagine we are researchers and we have to create a data management plan for every project which we are participating in. Otherwise, we will not be able to get a subsidy. A data management plan is a formal document that outlines how data is handled [1]. It covers two phases - a phase during a research project and a phase after the project is completed. Because data stewardship is not our main interest (we are for example natural scientists), we have no clue how we

© Springer Nature Switzerland AG 2019
R. Pergl et al. (Eds.): EOMAS 2019, LNBIP 366, pp. 70–81, 2019.
https://doi.org/10.1007/978-3-030-35646-0_6

should create a data management plan. However, because we are smart, we will somehow figure it out. We will learn about current legislative, best practices and we will create one data management plan and successfully submit it. Because it took a huge effort to assemble this document, we will reuse it and create a few copies of it for our additional subsidies. So we will use the document as a template for creating additional documents. However, because the world is changing, we may find that we have to change the data management plan. The change can be a correction of some error which we did, new legislation or new requirements, etc. Generally, a change in the content of a document can appear. However, it may also happen that we fail in a getting subsidy from one founder. Then we would like to apply for a subsidy in another founder. However, his structure of a data management plan is a little bit different. He requires the same information but in a different form. If we want to apply for his subsidy, again we have to rewrite a whole document. So the second type of change is just changing a document template or structure without changing an actual content of the document.

These two types of changes are not very good supported in traditional documents despite that we encounter this problem very often in our lives. This leads to the fact that traditional documents are very bad in term of evolvability.

In this paper, we would like to offer an approach to solve that which is based on Normalized System Theory [8]. In theory, evolvability is defined by the absence of combinatorial effects. A combinatorial effect is then defined a change whose impact is not solely related just to the kind of the change but also to the size of the system on which the change is applied on. So our approach should decrease these combinatorial effects and therefore make documents more evolvable. Our approach will be compared with an application of NS Theory in software development. This application has already proved that principles and recommendations in NS Theory help the system to be more evolvable. Further, our approach will be shown on an example of creating an evolvable document of a data management plan.

2 Related Work

2.1 Normalized Systems Theory

The core of Normalized Systems Theory [8] is to deal with evolvability of systems. It highlights modularity as one of the aspects when most systems fail, and therefore they have low evolvability. The modularity should be very high according to the theory. The theory exactly says: "The system should be composed of very fine-graded modules". If we break this rule more "combinatorial effects" may appear. To have combinatorial effects in the system means that the size of the change also depends on the size of the system. So our goal is to reduce the number of these effects to a minimum. Otherwise, the cost of the change could be very high.

NS Theory is based on 4 principles - *Separation of Concerns*, *Data Version Transparency*, *Action Version Transparency*, and *Separation of States*. In a domain of documents, only the first two principles are applicable, because the second two principles are workflow-related [10,12].

- *Separation of Concerns* states that we should separate all concerns from each other.
- *Data Version Transparency* states that each module should be updatable without any impact on others linked module

The NS Theory was originally invented mainly for information systems and software development [9]. But because the theory is very abstract, it has been successfully applied also to other domains, such as requirements engineering [13], study programs [11], etc.

2.2   Template and Styles

The problem of splitting actual content of the document and graphical design of the document was partly addressed for example by HyperText Markup Language (HTML) and Cascading Style Sheets (CSS). However, the separation was just on a level of graphical design. We can style the document, we can even hide some parts with CSS, but when we want to change the structure of the document (not its content, just a form), we have a problem.

2.3   Template Engine

Especially in web development, we can find many frameworks which offer to dynamically generate pages (documents) from user's defined templates. They offer to create smaller templates and then compose them together. This allows reusing some common parts in more documents. Further, they have a parameterization which gives you an option to passed some data into the template. Then the template engine generates the desired document which is influenced by parameters which passed in. This approach offers great modularity. However, the separation of concerns is still violated here because the templates are mixing both the actual content and the form of the document (document template) together.

2.4   Darwin Information Typing Architecture (DITA)

Darwin Information Typing Architecture (DITA) is an open standard for writing modular technical documentation [5]. It was developed by IBM in 2001. It enables to reuse common parts ("topics" in context of DITA) and assemble a document from that parts. It has an ability for making conditions in text. This means that you can distinguish between, for example, experts and normal users (e.g., you can include more information to the version for experts). The target audience of this technology are companies which need to maintain thousands of pages of their documentation. On the other hand, if we would like to apply this technology to the case of a user which wants to create a data management plan, of course, his need is to reuse some parts, but moreover, he needs to add his inputs to the document. This feature is not well supported in DITA because this tool was not designed for that.

2.5 Document Management Environment (DME)

Document Management Environment (DME) is an extension to the Microsoft Word. It should help users to designate any arbitrary document part as a template's variation point that can be customized to produce a specific document [6]. It identifies two roles - Document Senior Architect Clerk and Document Developer Clerk. The first one is designated to create and refine user guide templates. The second one is designed to create customizations of document for concrete clients. The core thing, which this tool adds over the DITA, is that it allows document customizations. DITA allows just to create document fragments, compose them, and based on some conditions, it allows to expand the desired document. It does not have any mechanism which would cover the problem of specific customization.

3 Violations of NS Theory in Traditional Documents

We assume that if we want to improve the evolvability of documents, we should adhere to the principles and recommendations of the NS Theory. In term of traditional documents, we can find several violations.

3.1 Separation of Concerns

The first principle is violated by combining the content of a document with a document template together. In some document editors, we mix it also with the style of the document. Putting these two (three) concerns together violates the first principle.

In the introduction, we mentioned an example with data management plan document. Imagine, we finalized a data management plan, and we submit it to a funder in terms to get a subsidy. However, the funder refused us, so we want to apply for a subsidy in a different funder. The content of the document is the same, but the funder has a different template. So we have to manually create a copy of the document, change the structure, reformulate parts of the documents, etc. Just because the content and the form are combined together and we are unable to exchange just one part. The big disadvantage of this approach is that we lost all the connection between the old and new document. If we want to add something in the future, we have to edit it in 2 places. That increases the combinatorial effects too.

3.2 Modularity

NS Theory assumes the evolvable system is composed of very fined-grade modules. That is the exact opposite of traditional monolithic documents where all parts are merged together. The result is that we can not easily reuse parts of the document. If we have more documents which share some part we cannot easily edit this shared part in one place. That increases combinatorial effects.

Back to our example, we have several data management plans which are the same in content but have different forms (structure, formatting, etc.). Sometimes we changed something, and we need to reflect it in our documents. Our only way is to change it in all documents manually. It is obvious that the effort increases together with a number of documents. So the size of the change is not constant. It does not depend just on the size of the change. It also depends on the number of affected documents.

4 Design Evolvable Documents

To build a generic technique for the evolvable document would be a quite hard issue. As far we are in the beginning, we restrict the domain to just a subset of all types of documents. We target types of documents which looks like a data management plan from our example. These documents are mostly contracts, applications, reports or legal documents. They serve as formal documents. They are well structured, and the structure is predefined. They are used in our everyday life, and we have to write them manually.

As we already discussed in Violation of NS Theory (Sect. 3), manual writing in document editor is not very evolvable. Moreover, for creating these specific types of documents, we have to be an expert in law or data stewardship domain. Otherwise, we are unable to create them because it is very hard to formulate sentences on our own about something where we are mostly not good at it. Our approach will also help with this aspect, but mainly it is focused on the problem of evolvability.

4.1 Separate Concerns

We split the process of creating document into three main parts - gathering information from a user, specifying document template and generating (expanding) target document (Fig. 1). First two parts are intended for users, so we are focusing on evolvability there. The last part is done automatically by a computer, so we do not have to take care of evolvability there because it is already evolvable (it does not require any inputs from us, so if some change appears, it could be just regenerated).

The first part (gathering information) is split into three additional sub-parts - a metamodel, a knowledge model and a knowledge. Each part should be evolvable by itself. In this paper, we would like to design the desired process. In the next papers, we would like to focus on the evolvability of each part separately.

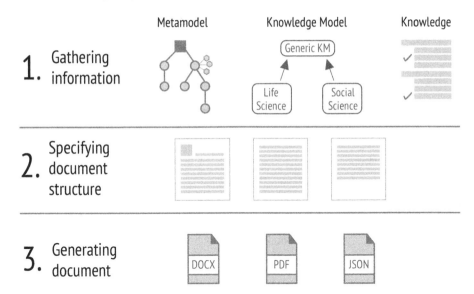

Fig. 1. Process overview

4.2   The Metamodel

NS Theory assumes that we build a whole system (document) from NS Elements. When we look into an application of NS Theory in software development [9], these elements are represented by data, task, connector, flow, and trigger element.

In our application, NS Elements are individual parts of the metamodel. The core of the metamodel are questions and answers. They are grouped in chapters and also linked together. So the resulting structure is a tree. The tree is structured from more general questions in the top to a more specific and detail questions in the bottom.

Due to being able to get the right answer from the user, every question can have a link to an expert. The question can also have references to related information and documents, websites or chapter from books which may help users to fill a right answer too.

The metamodel also offers to define metrics which can measure useful information about the result document. When we go back to our example, we talked about data management plans. There exists metrics which describe how good our data is managed - F.A.I.R. [14]. By answering questions about data stewardship, we can get a view on how a user take care of his data, and we can evaluate him. Moreover, we can even teach him how to do it better.

4.3   Knowledge Model

A knowledge model is composed of metamodel elements (NS Elements). For each type of document, we have a specific knowledge model, e.g., a data management

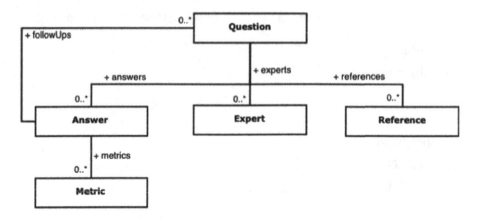

Fig. 2. Metamodel

plan, a rental contract, etc. We try to capture the knowledge about a specific domain and provide all questions about the actual topic. This does not mean that the user has to answer all of them. By choosing answers, we will show him just right sub-parts of the tree which are relevant to him (Fig. 2).

It is unrealistic to think we can create one generic knowledge model which would cover a whole topic and would be shared across all users and organizations. So it would be nice to have a mechanism for customizing the original generic knowledge model (Fig. 3). Organizations may have special needs. In our example with data management plans, organizations in natural science may want to add more specific questions for their branch or remove some questions which are not valid for them.

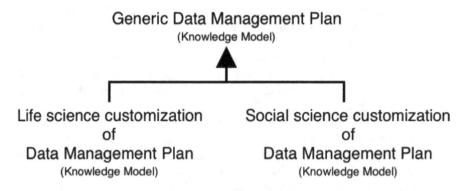

Fig. 3. Hierarchy of Knowledge Models (including generic knowledge model and its customizations)

Because customized knowledge model lives its own life, it can become outdated. So there should be a mechanism of how to apply changes from generic knowledge model to the forked knowledge model as far as we want to stay evolvable. This means that we should guarantee that the customizations are evolvable in time.

We assume that this subpart of our process will evolve the most. Therefore we started with the solving evolvability here as a first. More details about the migration process of customized knowledge model can be found in Vojtech Knaisl's diploma thesis [7].

4.4   Knowledge

Knowledge is gathered from the user's answers. As we have already mentioned, the user does not have to answer all the questions. Based on his answers, we show him another question which is relevant to him.

Compares to traditional document where the knowledge is spread over the whole document, here we have a good granularity so we can better perform some metrics on the knowledge and give user feedback. This is an example that our approach is better machine-actionable compares to unstructured documents. This may be used in the future as a great benefit.

We can see that it is easy to do a modification of knowledge like changing user's answer because all we have to do then is to just re-expand the document. So the cost of the change here (e.g., changing user's answers) depends just on how many answers we want to change and does not have any connection to the size of the expanded document. If we have more dependent document templates, we can re-expand them all and get desired documents. We can observe that we got rid of the combinatorial effects in this situation. Because normally, we would have to rewrite parts in many documents which would be intellectually and administratively unmanageable.

When we return to the application of NS Theory in software, the knowledge model and the knowledge can be compared to a model where desired software is defined. From that software model, the desired application is then expanded. Same as we expand the desired document from the knowledge model and the knowledge.

However, one problem remains here. The knowledge belongs to a specific version of the knowledge model. When we upgrade the knowledge model, we have also to upgrade our knowledge. This challenge is currently in front of us. However, the great benefit here is that all data is well structured so we can engage computer to do the migration progress automatically.

4.5   Document Template

The document template serves for a composition of a target document together. It makes a view on knowledge gathered from a user, and together with document template which relates to some knowledge model, it creates the desired document. Further, it offers a space to do specific customization. Back to our example with data management plans, each founding agency can have a specific structure of a document, branding, etc. The agency may want to add to all their documents some common header part, static text, etc. The document template should be able to cover all these special needs.

Because of these extensions, we need to do a special migration process. When we want to upgrade to a newer version, we have to do a harvest. It gathers all our texts, images, etc., migrates to a newer template and then applies the customization back to the template.

In the application of NS Theory in software development, this part is related to the writing NS Customization to expanded code. It has the same goal - to define a custom logic which can not be covered in the model. During the upgrade, we can see there the same process as we have in our template. We need to harvest the customized code, re-expand the newer model and put back the customized code.

4.6   Separated Responsibility

In the process of creating a document, they are involved two kinds of users - domain experts (e.g., data stewards, lawyers) and normal users (researchers who want to create a data management plan, owners of an apartment who wants to sign a rental contract). This split of roles guarantees better guidance for normal users who are not well educated for example in data stewardship domain. Knowledge models are mainly created by domain experts the same as document templates. Filling knowledge models with actual knowledge are then left to users.

4.7   Version Management

To be able to do a proper migration process, all parts and sub-parts of the whole process have their versions, or they depend on a specific version of other part or sub-part. Here is a list for a recapitulation:

- *Metamodel*
    - has its own version
    - does not depend on anything
- *Knowledge Model*
    - has its own version
    - depends on version of the metamodel
- *Knowledge*
    - does not have has its own version
    - depends on version of the knowledge model
- *Document Template*
    - does not have its own version
    - depends on version of the knowledge model

5   Applying in Practice

To evaluate our approach in practice, we create an application which should demonstrate our proposal [2]. We chose a data stewardship domain and create a knowledge model for a data management plan. Currently, the web application has implemented just a subset of all proposed functions which we mentioned here. We may create a knowledge model or create its customization, fill it with the knowledge, edit document template and then generate the document. Migrations are almost missing there. This application is published as an open source [4]. Our goal is to test there our approach in practice. Further, we start one instance as a demo where everyone can play with knowledge models and documents [3]. Currently, it has about 180 users from 112 institutions from whom we got mostly positive feedback.

6   Conclusion

Our approach was to deal with low evolvability of traditional monolithic documents. We focused just on a subset of all documents where we try to improve evolvability. We designed the architecture, and we tried to apply it in practice. We may say that we were successful. We can claim (according to the results in practice) that the number of combinatorial effects was reduced and generated documents are more evolvable.

6.1   Future Work

Our plan for the future is to design migration processes between all parts and sub-parts of the process. The list of needed migrations is here:

1. **Metamodel → Knowledge Model**
    - *Description:* a structure of the metamodel may change. After the change, it is needed to change all dependent knowledge model
    - *State:* in planning
2. **Generic Knowledge Model → Customized Knowledge Model**
    - *Description:* we may fork a generic knowledge model and create a customized knowledge model. So we have two knowledge model which evolves separately. However, to keep our customized knowledge model up to date, we may want to upgrade it with new changes from the generic knowledge model.
    - *State:* the first simple version was implemented in Vojtech Knaisl's diploma thesis [7]
3. **Knowledge Model → Knowledge**
    - *Description:* we filled our knowledge model with answers (knowledge). Then we decided to change the knowledge model. So our knowledge is outdated. We want to upgrade it with changes which come from a newer version of the knowledge model.
    - *State:* in planning

4. Knowledge Model → Document Template

- *Description:* we create our custom document template for a specific knowledge model. The knowledge model changed. We may want to upgrade the document template in terms to keep it up to date.
- *State:* in planning

Except for the migration processes, we will focus on the document template and how to structure it. Currently, our approach is to put as most things as we can to the knowledge model. The reason is that the knowledge model is very good in evolvability. However, the result is that the target document is not as human-readable as it could be. So it will be a big challenge to make it more human-readable.

Acknowledgment. This research was supported by the grant of Czech Technical University in Prague No. SGS17/211/OHK3/3T/18. The work on the Data Stewardship Wizard is partially funded by IOCB of the CAS and ELIXIR infrastructure.

References

1. Data management plan. https://library.stanford.edu/research/data-management-services/data-management-plans. Accessed 13 Mar 2019
2. Data stewardship wizard. https://ds-wizard.org. Accessed 13 Mar 2019
3. Demo instance of data stewardship wizard. https://app.ds-wizard.org. Accessed 13 Mar 2019
4. Github repository for data stewardship wizard. http://github.com/ds-wizard. Accessed 13 Mar 2019
5. Harrison, N.: The Darwin information typing architecture (DITA): applications for globalization. In: Proceedings of the International Professional Communication Conference, IPCC 2005, pp. 115–121 (2005). https://doi.org/10.1109/IPCC.2005.1494167
6. Jarzabek, S., Dan, D.: Documentation management environment for software product lines. In: 2017 Federated Conference on Computer Science and Information Systems (FedCSIS), pp. 1325–1334 (2017). https://doi.org/10.15439/2017F106
7. Knaisl, V.: Migration tool for data stewardship knowledge model. Master's thesis, Czech Technical University in Prague, Faculty of Information Technology (2018)
8. Mannaert, H., Verelst, J., De Bruyn, P.: Normalized Systems theory: from foundations for evolvable software toward a general theory for evolvable design
9. Oorts, G., Huysmans, P., Bruyn, P.D., Mannaert, H., Verelst, J., Oost, A.: Building evolvable software using normalized systems theory: a case study. In: 2014 47th Hawaii International Conference on System Sciences, pp. 4760–4769 (2014). https://doi.org/10.1109/HICSS.2014.585
10. Oorts, G., Mannaert, H., De Bruyn, P.: Exploring design aspects of modular and evolvable document management. In: Aveiro, D., Pergl, R., Guizzardi, G., Almeida, J.P., Magalhães, R., Lekkerkerk, H. (eds.) EEWC 2017. LNBIP, vol. 284, pp. 126–140. Springer, Cham (2017). https://doi.org/10.1007/978-3-319-57955-9_10
11. Oorts, G., Mannaert, H., De Bruyn, P., Franquet, I.: On the evolvable and traceable design of (under)graduate education programs. In: Aveiro, D., Pergl, R., Gouveia, D. (eds.) EEWC 2016. LNBIP, vol. 252, pp. 86–100. Springer, Cham (2016). https://doi.org/10.1007/978-3-319-39567-8_6

12. Suchánek, M., Pergl, R.: Evolvable documents - an initial conceptualization, pp. 39–44. IARIA
13. Verelst, J., Silva, A.R., Mannaert, H., Ferreira, D.A., Huysmans, P.: Identifying combinatorial effects in requirements engineering. In: Proper, H.A., Aveiro, D., Gaaloul, K. (eds.) EEWC 2013. LNBIP, vol. 146, pp. 88–102. Springer, Heidelberg (2013). https://doi.org/10.1007/978-3-642-38117-1_7
14. Wilkinson, M.D., et al.: The FAIR guiding principles for scientific data management and stewardship. Sci. Data **3**, 160,018 (2016). https://doi.org/10.1038/sdata.2016.18

Mapping UFO-B to BPMN, BORM, and UML Activity Diagram

Marek Suchánek$^{(\boxtimes)}$ and Robert Pergl

Faculty of Information Technology, Czech Technical University in Prague,
16000 Prague 6, Czech Republic
{marek.suchanek,robert.pergl}@fit.cvut.cz

Abstract. Process modelling is the key part of a problem domain analysis, and there are multiple modelling languages for that purpose. In this paper, we present the mapping of three of such languages – namely BPMN, BORM, and UML Activity Diagram – with Unified Foundational Ontology UFO, more specifically its part describing behavioural aspects called UFO-B. Due to the mapping, we were able to find out interesting similarities and options when working with the selected languages and we also compare them in terms of expressiveness with respect to UFO. The specific properties of each languages became even more highlighted and explained, so this comparison can be used for a decision which language to use in a particular case. Our contribution can be used for future work in models integrations and transformations.

Keywords: Unified foundational ontology · BPMN · BORM · UML Activity Diagram · Ontology mapping

1 Introduction

In software and business engineering, the ontologies and structural conceptual models together with process modelling, are being used more or less separately. During recent years, more and more effort is put into integrating these two approaches as their goal is the same – to describe various aspects of a system or a domain [12]. One of the notable examples of this initiative is ontology-driven conceptual modelling language OntoUML based on the Unified Foundational Ontology (UFO).

UFO covers modelling of structural aspects (UFO-A) and behavioural aspects (UFO-B). There are already process modelling languages that are widely used for modelling behaviour of systems and domains such as UML, BPMN, or BORM. Finding a mapping between these languages and the UFO-B ontology could bring more ontological insight into the existing languages and potentially help with models integration. It can provide an overview and comparison of their expressiveness, i.e., what they can capture in terms of conceptual modelling of behaviour.

R. Pergl et al. (Eds.): EOMAS 2019, LNBIP 366, pp. 82–98, 2019.
https://doi.org/10.1007/978-3-030-35646-0_7

Our goal in this research is to find such matches between the UFO-B ontology and BPMN, BORM, and UML Activity diagrams and to discuss possibilities, their mutual advantages and disadvantages in situations where the mapping is not evident and unambiguous directly. This work is part of a more massive endeavour to achieve an integration framework for various conceptual, as well as process modelling languages for capturing different aspects of the problem domain. As a side product, it should also allow conversions between models.

First, we quickly go through the needed related work in Sect. 2, we clarify the necessary terminological background, Unified Foundational Ontology and process modelling languages that we want to map with UFO-B. We investigate briefly possibilities of doing such ontological mappings based on already existing examples. Then, we apply this knowledge in Sect. 3 which is split into parts where we set requirements, then design the mapping for the modelling languages and finally we summarise in a comparison. After that, in Sect. 4, we evaluate our work from various aspects. In Sect. 5, we suggest possible follow-up research, as well as the use of our contribution in practice.

2   Related Work and Terminology

In this section, we briefly describe the current state-of-the-art in process modelling and its key purpose together with the selected modelling languages. Then there is a basic information about UFO, its most recent development, and summary of the UFO-B terms that we use for the mapping.

2.1   Process Modelling

Process modelling is used similarly to other types of conceptual modelling to capture aspects of a system called *problem domain*. For process modelling, the aspects are behavioural, i.e., how people, machines, and other participants work together in order to transform some inputs to outputs in a repeatable way. It can capture the workflow in different levels of detail and cover also related parts such as communication by artefacts or signals, timed events, intermediate states, and so on. Process modelling languages historically originate from basic flow charts, state machines, and Petri nets; therefore, they are never totally disjunct, and significant similarities are well-observable. [26]

Usually, process models can be used for business analysis and optimizations in terms of the Capability Maturity Model (CMM) or for understanding the domain to develop a software system [16]. For software engineering, process models can be often used for simulations or even orchestrations [19]. There are process systems that use configurable workflows to notify users, gather data, process them, and pass them to other services or users according to defined steps. Process engineering is an important discipline for both business and software analysis. [19]

2.2 BPMN

Business Process Model and Notation (BPMN) is not just a notation but a set of principles and rules for the description of business processes [9]. Process modelling methods are defined over and using BPMN [23]. It is standardised by OMG and therefore tooling, and process orchestrators using Business Process Execution Language (BPEL) together with the notation are widely used [24]. BPMN in its version 2.0 uses stable metamodel called BPDM for a consistent language. Due to that, XML schemas exist for BPMN models transformation for decision making and other applications within organisation systems [1]. When relating BPMN with UFO ontology, there is a research [13] that proposes "Onto-BPMN" as a process ontology-driven language.

BPMN models can be seen as more complex flow charts [25]. Among others, it introduces swimlines called pools and activities of several types. Activities can also contain a subprocess enabling modularity. Not only activities have defined types (based on its nature concerning processing), but also multiple types of events and gateways are defined. In the BPMN standard, conditional events, timed events, errors, and signals are defined. For gateways, instead of traditional decision branching and parallel fork, there are parallel, inclusive, exclusive, sophisticated and event-based gateways [2]. The notation also allows associations and message flows (as a complement to sequence flow between activities) and artefacts of types: data objects, groups, and annotations [1].

2.3 UML

The universal Unified Modeling Language (UML) [21] provides several types of diagrams, and there is the behavioural group of them. It contains diagrams such as use case diagram, state machine diagram, object/class interaction diagrams, and the activity diagram. For process modelling of a domain level, the Activity Diagram offers the broadest assortment of constructs; others are more focused on specific aspects of behaviour [5]. The Activity Diagram can be used even as a workflow specification language, albeit a simple one [4].

In the UML Activity Diagram (UML AD) [21], there are swimlines for actors, then their actions and activities, initial and end state. It supports decisions, parallel forking, timing, sending and receiving messages, and it can also be bound to states of objects modelled with state machine diagram. The activities can be composed, so one activity represents whole "packed" process, enabling reusability and modularity. [7] shows that there is considerable overlap between UML AD and BPMN, but BPMN provides a standard way of transformation to the BPEL execution language and some symbols in BPMN can be substituted only by multiple in UML AD, i.e., BPMN has higher expressiveness.

2.4 BORM

Business Objects Relation Modelling (BORM) is another process-modelling method that is less-known than BPMN or UML AD, but on the other hand, it introduces interesting concepts. When compared to them, it provides a simpler notation, but practice suggests that it is conceptually sufficient for describing complex business processes in many situations. It is tied with object-oriented analysis of a system and based on the formalism of communicating state machines [17]. Model-driven engineering (MDE) is well supported in BORM, and it provides modularity [22]. There are two types of diagrams. The first is Object Relations (OR) diagram, which is used for process modelling as shown on a simple example in Fig. 1. The second one is the Business Architecture (BA) diagram, and it can be used to model the modules of a system or business domain and attach scenarios related to OR diagrams. [17]

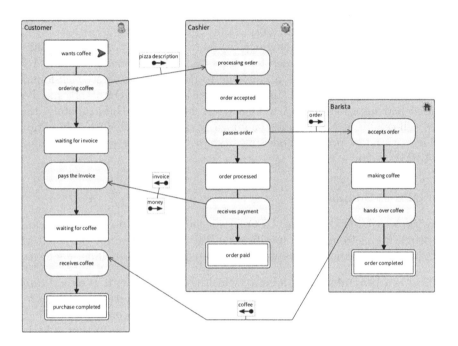

Fig. 1. Example of BORM OR diagram – a café

BORM, similarly to the majority of process modelling languages, can be seen as an improved and formalised flowchart. Instead of swimlines or pools, participant "blocks" are used with a type – human, organisation, or technology. Each participant has its state machine where states are separated by activities acting as transitions. Similarly to UML AD and BORM, a state can contain a nested state machine. Participants can influence each other only by sending messages from their activities. Branching and forking is done without any other constructs (gateways), just using conditional transitions and states. [17]

Although BORM is in its essence a combination of several UML diagrams (Activity, Sequence and State Machine), we investigate it in this paper as a separate language. We hypothesise that mappings of BORM and UML AD will be very similar, and the more significant difference will be in the case of mapping to BPMN.

2.5 Unified Foundational Ontology

The Unified Foundational Ontology (UFO) is an upper ontology that describes "high-level" terms such as *ObjectType*, *Agent*, *Entity*, or *Event*. It creates a hierarchy of these terms and its relations, which can be used in lower ontologies to describe a problem domain together with the defined constraints. It is separated into three parts: UFO-A – structural aspects, UFO-B – behavioural aspects, and UFO-C – social aspects. UFO is maintained by its author Giancarlo Guizzardi and the NEMO research group. [10]

For UFO-A, there is a language – more specifically a UML profile – OntoUML that uses stereotypes for classes and associations to denote UFO concepts. As such, it provides a language to design ontologically well-founded structural conceptual models. In a recent work [11], the OntoUML has been revisited and improved as a new OntoUML 2.0 version. Unfortunately, there is no well-established modelling language so tightly related to foundational ontologies to allow process modelling despite the existing research, including OntoBPMN [8,20].

2.6 UFO-B Summary

For work with UFO (including UFO-B) specification, we use the specification and visualisations from online specification [14]. Here we describe the core terms briefly that will be then analysed in the selected process modelling languages:

- *Event* is a *perdurant*, i.e., an entity which occurs in time. It is either *atomic* or *complex*. Other perdurants are *object snapshot* (i.e. a state) and *situation*. An event is bounded in time using begin and end *time points*.
- *Atomic event* is type of event that is not intended to be further split into fragments. It always depends on an *object* and *manifestates* a *disposition*.
- *Complex event* is type of event that is composed of two or more events (*atomic* or *complex*) which are its parts.
- *Object* is an instance of an entity and is subtype of *endurant*, i.e., can be observed as a complete concept at any time point. Although it might change over time and at some point object is created and then it stops to exist. Therefore we can use *object snapshot* to capture how the object looked like at some point of time.
- *Participation* as a special type of *event* which *exclusively depends on* the object participant and *is participation of* another object. Subclasses of participations are object creation, change, and deletion.
- *Situation* is a snapshot of object states valid in the given temporal range, i.e., it captures values of objects during certain time period. It *triggers* an event which *brings about* a new situation which forms pre/post-situation relations.

A situation is *obtained in* a certain *time point*. There are derived relations *causes* and *directly causes* between two events where the first brings a situation causing the other directly or via more events and situations – capturing the causality between events.

– *Fact* is a special type of situation that is bound to exactly one time point. For situation this relationship is not mandatory.

– *Disposition* is an property of a situation (*is activated by situation*) and can be *manifested in* an atomic event. It can be understood as an "enabler" of following event.

To improve understanding and work with the UFO-B specification, we compiled the models introduced already in UFO-B paper [14] and made aggregated and convenient UML class diagrams depicting the previous description. First, Fig. 2 shows situations and dispositions, i.e, state at some point of time. Then, in Fig. 3 events are described with its subtypes and relations to situations and dispositions.

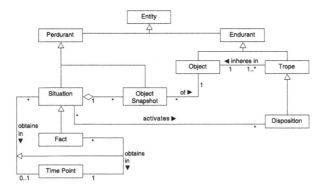

Fig. 2. Situations and dispositions in UFO-B (according to [18])

3 Our Approach

In this section, we apply knowledge of UFO-B and map its terms to constructs of the selected process modelling languages. Initially, we describe the methodological steps for each language to achieve our goals and to be able to compare the results afterwards.

3.1 Mapping Procedure

For each of the selected languages, we explain for each of the previously described UFO-B terms which modelling constructs could be used and how to achieve the match. Basically, there can be the following situations:

– there is a 1:1 match between a construct and a term, i.e. a semantic equivalence,

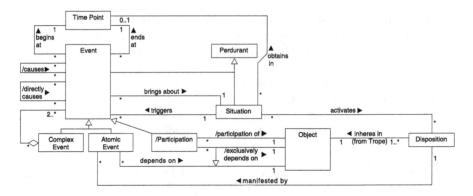

Fig. 3. Events in UFO-B (according to [18])

- a construct from the language is capturing something that UFO-B describes
  by multiple constructs,
- multiple constructs from the language must be used to capture a single term
  defined in UFO-B (opposite to the previous),
- the modelling language construct is out of the scope of UFO-B ontology or
  some UFO-B term is not covered.

Potentially, there can be more mapping options, and we will describe all
found. In the ideal case, all terms would be semantically equivalent with language
constructs, and all would be covered, i.e., mathematically speaking a bijection
between UFO-B terms and language constructs. After this formalised description, we will be able to compare how each language fits UFO-B and what special
construct has that cannot be mapped.

3.2   BPMN Analysis

We depict mapped terms of UFO-B to BPMN constructs in Fig. 4. Further explanation follows to describe the mapping in higher detail.

Event. The BPMN 2.0 notation offers three types of flow objects: *event*, *activity*,
and *gateway*. All of them occur between time points. Events are simple and
typed, e.g., signal, timed, or message, and they can be start, end, or intermediate.
They denote that some atomic thing happens or is being awaited. In a similar
way work the gateways, they are also atomic and of several types, for instance,
exclusive, parallel, or complex. But they serve just to split the flow conditionally
or using some defined strategy. Activities in BPMN are the real events that
actually do some work in the workflow. *Task* is a single activity that is not
structured further, therefore it is mapped to an atomic event together with
events and gateways. A complex event is represented by *subprocess* activity that
can contain a new flow but it is important that this flow cannot contain pools

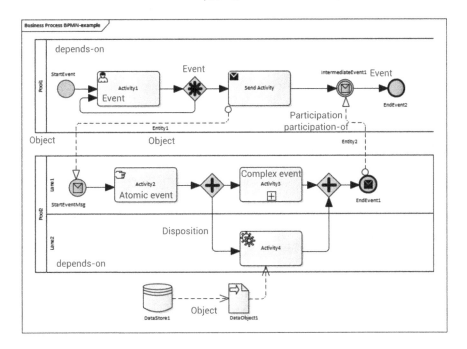

Fig. 4. Summary of UFO-B to BPMN mapping

and interact out of the borders. The pool captures the depends-on relation, i.e., an event, an activity, or a gateway depends on its executor (object) given by the *pool* and its *lane* in which it belongs to.

Object and Snapshot. There is no way of modelling object structure in the BPMN, but there are *data objects* that represent inputs and outputs of activities. They can also have a meaning of a *state*, which can change in the process. These objects can be stored in a *data store* that represents a sort of a database or a collection of objects of the same type.

Participation. It tempts to say that the participation from UFO-B is matching *pool/lane* capturing who "does" the activity but it would not fit with exclusively-depends-on and participation-of relations that are both mandatory and exactly with one object. A better match could be the usage of a *data object in activity* with a problem, that it is not constrained in BPMN to just one object, but multiple ones can be connected to an activity.

Situation and Fact. Situations should capture the current state in the flow. Since there is actually nothing to capture because no "internals" of objects are available in basic BPMN, we match situation to states that should be on each end of flow object, i.e., after a *flow object* is finished. Surely, it is brought-about

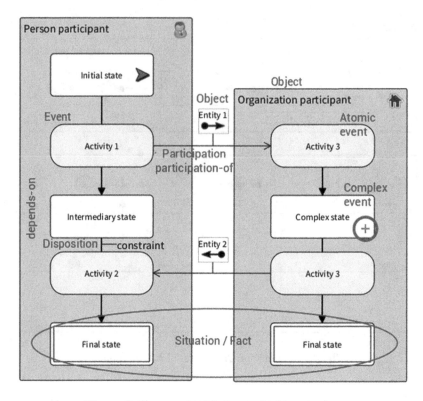

Fig. 5. Summary of UFO-B to BORM mapping

by the *flow event* which we map to UFO-B's event, and it triggers following flow events connected by a flow link. No bounding to time point is available, so facts cannot be captured clearly.

Disposition. According to the previous, a situation is close to BPMN's *flow object endpoint*, the disposition as a thing that is activated by situation should be a *flow link* which connects flow objects. It captures that if some flow object is done, e.g., a task is completed, an event proceeds or decision is made in a gateway, there is possible to continue with the next one. The manifested-by relation then means that the flow was used, but in BPMN, it violates restriction to manifesting only atomic events because it can relate subprocess activity, which we identified as the complex event.

3.3   BORM Analysis

Matching terms of UFO-B with BORM OR diagram are shown in Fig. 5. Business architecture diagram in BORM provides only modelling of structure and relations between scenarios as explained in the following subsections.

Event. There is only one construct that represents, and that is the *activity*. It cannot be further split into parts; therefore, it is mapped to the atomic event. It is more complicated with the complex event in BORM because it allows subprocess within a single state of a role or including activity inside a state. The state of BORM in our mapping represents partially perdurant – there can be an included activity or a subprocess as it is the complex event – but also endurant – it snapshots the state of its participant.

Object and Snapshot. As objects, there are participants and data flow objects used for the communication between them (more precisely between their activities). As the *data flow objects* are similar to BPMN, there is no modelling of their structure and states. On the other hand, *participants* are more detailed than in BPMN and allow associations and IS-A hierarchy to be captured. The states allow snapshotting an object, the internal structure can be described in BORM using ORD, but it is mostly omitted for the sake of clarity. Luckily, thanks to its object-oriented nature, it can be easily related to some class model that would be complementary and capture that.

Participation. Similarly to BPMN, activities as atomic events depends on the *participant*, and activities inside some of its state depend on him transitively. With the restriction that only one *communication* or a *data flow* that is incoming (exclusive) or outcoming is permitted per single activity, it corresponds to a participation of the other participant in the activity that belongs to the role of the first one.

Situation and Fact. The snapshots are modelled as states of participants, and then obviously, the situation is corresponding to a collection of *states*, where is at least one per participant's role. When there is a state of subprocess included in another state, that a "*substate*" is included as well. That indeed snapshots over the state in the process, but again it is not bounded to any time point, and distinction with the fact is not possible.

Disposition. A disposition in BORM is a property of a participant as it is mapped to an object that realises the *transitions* between states and activities. It is manifested when the transition is used to move in the flow or participants role. Some transitions might be conditional based on the state of participants which fits well with the definition in UFO-B – inheres in the object, e.g., its state in BORM.

3.4   UML Activity Diagram Analysis

Finally, Fig. 6 shows the mapping of UFO-B terms to UML AD according to following description of analysis.

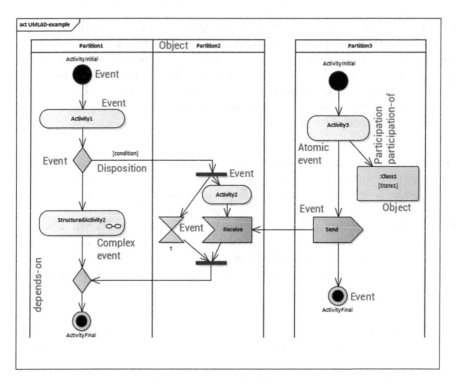

Fig. 6. Summary of UFO-B to UML Activity Diagram mapping

Event. The base of the UML Activity Diagram is an *activity* that represents the invocation of an operation, a step in a business process, or even an entire business process because they can be decomposed into *subactivities*. The *action* is a named element which represents a single atomic step within an activity, i.e. that is not further decomposed within the activity. This is analogical to events that are either complex or atomic. There are multiple predefined types of actions, such as send, receive, timed, and so on.

Object and Snapshot. In UML, multiple diagrams can be interlinked. Activity diagram can contain *objects* of *classes* from class diagrams with a defined *state* from related state machine diagram. Such an object can be passed between activities or just used in it or be created as a result. There are also *datastores* similarly to BPMN. And just as BPMN and BORM, there are *partitions* (or *swimlanes*) used for designating the executor of an activity or an action.

Participation. An object can participate in an activity or an action using an *object flow* connection. Again, for matching with UFO-B, restriction to maximally one object that participates in a single activity is required. Dependence between event and object from UFO-B is similarly to BPMN, and BORM captured using swimlanes.

Situation and Fact. Only states captured in the UML AD can be all individual states of *data objects*. For mapping situations from UFO-B, the activity ends can be used similarly to BPMN. Unluckily, there is no direct support for snapshotting the whole state of all used objects in the process, nor relating it to a time point. But semantically it is possible to create an *object model* representing the current state of the instances in the situation and link it to a point in time in UML AD (before or after an activity).

Disposition. Dispositions are closest to the places from which *control flow* links can go, i.e., end of activity or control nodes (initial, decision, fork, merge, etc.). It shows what next events can happen an eventually be manifested when decision is made, a flow splits to parallel or it just simply continues.

3.5   A Comparison of the Analysed Languages

According to the previous analysis of UFO-B terms in the selected process modelling languages, we were able to create a summary in Table 1. Some terms are nicely matching modelling constructs, for example, events with its complex and atomic subtypes have corresponding elements for modelling, but both BPMN and UML AD provide even further specialised subtypes with defined semantics and different symbols (such as timing or sending/receiving signals). In all three languages, event dependence is captured using its executor, and only naming differs – a pool with lanes, role, or partition – commonly known as swimlanes.

Participation as a particular type of event can be understood as including an external object in an event in process modelling. Is it possible, but for compliance restriction to just one incoming/outgoing object is necessary and it also seems as good design approach in process modelling (otherwise the event would be very complex, i.e., Separation of Concerns violation). None of the analysed languages provides explicit capturing of a time point when the event or state starts and ends. Due to that, we cannot distinguish between situation and fact of UFO-B, but a situation is related to states captured in process modelling after doing the event or before the very first one. Disposition is then realised by existing flow links between event-mapped elements (and states in case of BORM) that capture what events can be manifested next.

BPMN and UML AD are almost identical when mapping to UFO-B terms. The only crucial difference is that UML provides an easy way of diagrams integration and thanks to that, more details such as object structure, internal states, or snapshot in object diagram can be used. With this combination of diagrams, UML outcomes as the best match of three selected. If we strictly stay just with UML AD, then BORM is closer to UFO-B thanks to its inclusion of states in roles.

Table 1. Summary table of UFO-B mappings

UFO-B	BPMN	BORM	UML AD
Event	event, activity, gateway	activity	activity, action
- depends-on	pool/lane	role	partition
- Atomic	task	activity	action(s), simple activity
- Complex	subprocess	subprocess in state	structured activity
Object	participant, data object with state	participant, data flow	participant, data object, UML objects
Participation	event with attached object	event with attached object	event with attached object
- participation-of	message flow	data flow, communication	object links
Situation/Fact	activity end	state in all participants	activity end, UML Object Diagram
Disposition	flow links	flow	control links

4 Evaluation

Our contribution described in the previous section shows how the widely used process modelling languages can be mapped with a part of upper ontology UFO-B. Although the mapping is not bijective nor trivial or straightforward and loses details, it can be used to understand both languages and the ontology better. Its mapping allowed us to see the process modelling languages from a different perspective that will be useful for future work. Hypothetically, even terms from UFO-C [18] (including *Agent*, *Action*, and *performs* relation) could be used for mapping of process models.

We identified that the selected process modelling languages have more in common together than with the more generic UFO-B ontology. Examples are specific types of events or using different notions of participation. On the other hand, mapping with UFO-B allows continuing with using models in those process modelling languages as a complement to OntoUML (UFO-A) structural conceptual models. A better solution for the future might be to use the bottom-up approach instead of top-down and develop an intermediary ontology of process modelling languages merely using or integrating the selected terms from UFO-B and possibly other upper ontologies.

Surely as this research is very initial, it could be broadened by mapping more modelling languages that capture behaviour. Exciting and challenging would be mapping for slightly different approaches than "flow-charts", for example, using Design & Engineering Methodology for Organizations (DEMO) which is based on transactions [3] or ArchiMate with its behaviour aspects at business layer [26]. Also, the enterprise-oriented approach using multi-aspect models and metamodeling that would worth further analysis and mapping with UFO-B is Multi-perspective Enterprise Modelling (MEMO) [6].

Another enhancement in this way could be done by integrating different upper ontologies that describe behaviour as UFO-B, and therefore they should contain terms that overlap or have some other relation across ontologies, for example, specialisation or generalisation. That could allow broader integration and allow generating process models from a semantic description in those ontologies. More languages and ontologies adopted would also result in increased possibilities if there is a transformation mechanism that uses this mapping. Transforming models can result in loss of details since they are focused on different aspects and have different expressiveness. On the other hand, the mapping could also relate various process models made in distinct languages to provide a better description of a problem domain.

5   Future Work Ideas

Although the presented analysis presents just first, mostly informal observations, it shows how existing notations may be possibly enhanced in the direction of ontological clarity. We also briefly suggest some of the other possibilities.

5.1   Integration with Structural Models

To capture behaviour in process models, a related notion of the domain structure is needed, too. For example, actors performing actions, messages passed between them, or states in which actors are before and after activities are tied to the structure in the domains, i.e., concepts, properties, relations, and constraints. Our mapping can help with interconnecting process models made in mapped modelling languages with structural OntoUML models thanks to the relations between UFO-A and UFO-B.

As there are many process modelling languages, also multiple conceptual modelling languages for describing domain structure are available, for example, UML class diagram, Entity-Relationship, or Object Role Modelling (ORM) [15]. It could be a way to map those models similarly using an ontology, similarly to this analysis and then to integrate structural and behavioural ontologies. The ultimate goal to interconnect various models and provide a complex holistic view on a domain can be hypothetically achieved through that.

5.2   Business Case Analysis

Another related research could investigate the use of different modelling languages in real-world scenarios. Hypothetically, for various types of processes, different process modelling languages are more suitable, and its combination in overall domain description is needed. The research would need to propose a typology of such processes with a recommendation of modelling language using solid proofs. If that is not applicable, then it should explain why such typology is not possible and that there are more unbiased aspects involved in the selection of the language.

The immediate problem is that analysis would need non-trivial real-world business cases since any conclusion can be made based on a fictional case. However, acquiring multiple and well-modelled processes from business domains is hard to achieve because it is often part of corporate secrets. An option then could be to use processes from a public sector, but those are already very domain specific.

5.3   Process Modelling Generic Ontology

As more languages can be mapped, we might need more terms and relations that are not described in UFO-B to avoid losing important details in models. For that, a new generic ontology focused purely on process modelling could be developed. Of course, this approach would not mean leaving UFO-B and other foundational or even process-oriented ontologies – they should remain connected using relations between terms in different ontologies. It could lead to higher versatility and extensibility than with UFO-B as core vocabulary for the mappings.

6   Conclusion

In this paper, we presented our mapping of UFO-B terms with three process modelling languages – BPMN, BORM, and UML Activity Diagrams. It is visible from the description that the similarities between the languages are higher than with the UFO-B ontology terms that are more generic. Modelling languages often provide specialised types of events and actions over UFO-B, which are lost when matching with a more generic term. Nevertheless, our contribution is ready to be used for further research and used in practice, as we suggested in the future work section. This mapping is the first and foundational step for us in integrations of various process models.

Acknowledgements. This research was supported by the grant of Czech Technical University in Prague No. SGS17/211/OHK3/3T/18.

References

1. Allweyer, T.: BPMN 2.0: Introduction to the Standard for Business Process Modeling. BoD-Books on Demand, Norderstedt (2016)

2. Chinosi, M., Trombetta, A.: BPMN: an introduction to the standard. Comput. Stand. Interfaces **34**(1), 124–134 (2012)
3. Dietz, J.L., Hoogervorst, J.A.: Enterprise ontology in enterprise engineering. In: Proceedings of the 2008 ACM Symposium on Applied Computing, pp. 572–579. ACM (2008)
4. Dumas, M., ter Hofstede, A.H.M.: UML activity diagrams as a workflow specification language. In: Gogolla, M., Kobryn, C. (eds.) UML 2001. LNCS, vol. 2185, pp. 76–90. Springer, Heidelberg (2001). https://doi.org/10.1007/3-540-45441-1_7
5. Fowler, M.: UML Distilled: A Brief Guide to the Standard Object Modeling Language, 3rd edn. Addison-Wesley Professional, Reading (2003)
6. Frank, U.: Multi-perspective enterprise modeling (MEMO) conceptual framework and modeling languages, pp. 1258–1267. IEEE Computer Society (2002). https://doi.org/10.1109/HICSS.2002.993989
7. Geambaşu, C.V.: Bpmn vs uml activity diagram for business process modeling. Account. Manag. Inf. Syst. **11**(4), 637–651 (2012)
8. Ghidini, C., Rospocher, M., Serafini, L.: A formalisation of BPMN in description logics. Technical report, TR 06–004, FBK-irst (2008)
9. Group, O.M.: Business process modeling notation, version 2.0 (2011). https://www.omg.org/spec/BPMN/2.0
10. Guizzardi, G.: Ontological Foundations for Structural Conceptual Models. Centre for Telematics and Information Technology, Telematica Instituut, University of Twente, Enschede, The Netherlands (2005). http://doc.utwente.nl/50826/1/thesis_Guizzardi.pdf
11. Guizzardi, G., Fonseca, C.M., Benevides, A.B., Almeida, J.P.A., Porello, D., Sales, T.P.: Endurant types in ontology-driven conceptual modeling: towards OntoUML 2.0. In: Trujillo, J.C., Davis, K.C., Du, X., Li, Z., Ling, T.W., Li, G., Lee, M.L. (eds.) ER 2018. LNCS, vol. 11157, pp. 136–150. Springer, Cham (2018). https://doi.org/10.1007/978-3-030-00847-5_12
12. Guizzardi, G., Guarino, N., Almeida, J.P.A.: Ontological considerations about the representation of events and endurants in business models. In: La Rosa, M., Loos, P., Pastor, O. (eds.) BPM 2016. LNCS, vol. 9850, pp. 20–36. Springer, Cham (2016). https://doi.org/10.1007/978-3-319-45348-4_2
13. Guizzardi, G., Wagner, G.: Conceptual simulation modeling with Onto-UML. In: Proceedings of the Winter Simulation Conference, WSC 2012, pp. 5:1–5:15. Winter Simulation Conference (2012). http://dl.acm.org/citation.cfm?id=2429759.2429765
14. Guizzardi, G., Wagner, G., de Almeida Falbo, R., Guizzardi, R.S.S., Almeida, J.P.A.: Towards ontological foundations for the conceptual modeling of events. In: Ng, W., Storey, V.C., Trujillo, J.C. (eds.) ER 2013. LNCS, vol. 8217, pp. 327–341. Springer, Heidelberg (2013). https://doi.org/10.1007/978-3-642-41924-9_27
15. Halpin, T.: Comparing metamodels for ER, ORM and UML data models. In: Advanced Topics in Database Research, vol. 3, pp. 23–44. IGI Global (2004)
16. Jalote, P.: CMM in Practice. Pearson Education India (2000)
17. Knott, R., Merunka, V., Polák, J.: The BORM method: a third generation object-oriented methodology. In: Management of the Object-Oriented Development Process. IGI Global (2005)
18. Křemen, P.: Unified foundational ontology documentation (2018). http://onto.fel.cvut.cz/ontologies/ufo/. Accessed 25 Mar 2019
19. Laguna, M., Marklund, J.: Business Process Modeling, Simulation and Design. Chapman and Hall/CRC, Boca Raton (2018)

20. de Oliveira Bringuente, A.C., de Almeida Falbo, R., Guizzardi, G.: Using a foundational ontology for reengineering a software process ontology. J. Inf. Data Manag. **2**(3), 511 (2011)
21. (OMG), O.M.G.: OMG unified modeling language, v. 2.5. Technical report (2015). http://www.omg.org/spec/UML/2.5/PDF
22. Podloucký, M., Pergl, R., Kroha, P.: Revisiting the BORM OR diagram composition pattern. In: Barjis, J., Pergl, R., Babkin, E. (eds.) EOMAS 2015. LNBIP, vol. 231, pp. 102–113. Springer, Cham (2015). https://doi.org/10.1007/978-3-319-24626-0_8
23. Silver, B.: BPMN Method and Style, with BPMN Implementer's Guide: A Structured Approach for Business Process Modeling and Implementation Using BPMN 2.0. Cody-Cassidy Press, Aptos (2011)
24. Völzer, H.: An overview of BPMN 2.0 and its potential use. In: Mendling, J., Weidlich, M., Weske, M. (eds.) BPMN 2010. LNBIP, vol. 67, pp. 14–15. Springer, Heidelberg (2010). https://doi.org/10.1007/978-3-642-16298-5_3
25. Wahl, T., Sindre, G.: An analytical evaluation of bpmn using a semiotic quality framework. In: Advanced Topics in Database Research, vol. 5, pp. 94–105. IGI Global (2006)
26. Weske, M.: Business process management architectures. Business Process Management, pp. 333–371. Springer, Heidelberg (2012). https://doi.org/10.1007/978-3-642-28616-2_7

Exploration of Creativity Techniques
in Software Engineering
in Training-Application-Feedback Cycle

Anna E. Bobkowska[✉]

Gdańsk University of Technology, Narutowicza 11/12, 80-233 Gdańsk, Poland
annab@eti.pg.edu.pl

Abstract. Creativity research has proposed about a hundred and fifty creativity techniques. The question is whether they can be applied in software engineering for creativity training or directing creativity in software projects. This paper aims at answering this question via a quasi-experiment conducted in Training-Application-Feedback cycle in which participants express their opinions about selected creativity techniques after training and an attempt to apply them in software-related context.

Keywords: Creativity techniques · Software project · Quasi-experiment · Creativity training · Directed creativity

1 Introduction

In consequence of increasing demands for innovations there is a need for more creativity in software engineering. Creativity in technological context must deal with both novelty and value. While several myths still circulate in popular understanding of creativity, a certain level of control over creative processes seem to be necessary in technological applications. The most popular creativity techniques in software engineering are brainstorming and mind mapping. Most software engineers do not even suspect that other creativity techniques might exist.

In creativity research area, one can find about 150 creativity techniques [1–5], and one might wonder about the potential to apply them in software projects. Some techniques, e.g. drawings or tower building, have been already applied for creativity training, but their impact on creativity in software projects has not been confirmed. Therefore, one can pose the following questions: Which creativity techniques are useful for training software engineers? Which creativity techniques are useful for directing creativity in software projects? Which creativity techniques are useful for achieving particular effects related to creativity? What could be a frame of reference for managing creativity issues in software projects?

The goal of this paper is to explore applicability of creativity techniques in software engineering area. We take an interdisciplinary approach which uses results of creativity research. The fundamentals for this research are taken from research results conducted

© Springer Nature Switzerland AG 2019
R. Pergl et al. (Eds.): EOMAS 2019, LNBIP 366, pp. 99–118, 2019.
https://doi.org/10.1007/978-3-030-35646-0_8

by Polish creativity researchers [5, 6]. The empirical studies were conducted in Training-Application-Feedback cycle which allowed to acquire the feedback on selected creativity techniques after the creativity training with these techniques and an attempt to apply them to software-related issues.

The paper is structured as follows. An overview of background issues related to creativity in software development is presented in Sect. 2. The design of the quasi-experiment and some remarks on conduct of the studies are described in Sect. 3. The research results and their interpretation are presented in Sect. 4. Section 5 contains conclusions and prospects for further work.

2   Background: Creativity in Software Development

This paper's focus is on application of creativity techniques. However, it is useful to see this topic in a broader context of creativity in software development. Thus, the following sub-sections present:

- our approach to creativity studies in software project in terms of fundamentals of the framework, its dimensions and related work within the framework,
- results of literature review regarding creativity in software development which shows large diversity of topics and issues under studies,
- information about creativity techniques and discussion of their use in software project.

2.1   Framework for Creativity Studies in Software Project

Taking into account about 60 years of creativity research, it seems obvious that serious studies about creativity in software project should be interdisciplinary. They should integrate general knowledge about creativity with specifics of application in software engineering. Creativity research contains a huge number of results which have been formulated in a diversified context of discovery. So, the main question in the attempt of applying creativity research in software development area is whether these results are valid in the context of application to software development. On the other hand, creativity research literature commences respect and prevents from generating simplified or naive theories.

The framework includes macro-dimensions related to chapters from creativity research handbook [6] and micro-dimensions of creativity process resulting from research and practice related to directed creativity process [7]. They have been customized to specifics of software development with an attempt to integrate them with methodological approach in software engineering [8]. With this framework we have also published papers on creativity management [9], risk of creativity in software project [10] and dealing with positive risk of creativity in software project [11]. The following macro-dimensions structure the framework: product of creativity, creativity process (including use of creativity techniques), creative person, creative place (environment, organization), creativity mechanisms on cognitive level as well as dynamics of creativity in interdisciplinary teams. The micro-dimensions of creativity process consist of:

preparation phase (problem identification and analysis of related information), a phase of generating ideas, solution elaboration and validation of the solution.

Another characteristic feature of the framework is integration and balance between creative and methodological approaches in software project. Project manager, business analyst and user interface designer have more space for creativity (as their decisions have bigger impact on project or software product) than other roles which must deals with several technological constraints. An interesting issue is also interplay between software engineering techniques and creativity. Preparation phase of creativity is related to several software analysis techniques, solution elaboration phase can use specific software documentation and modeling methods, and validation of the solution can benefit from validation, testing and other software quality assurance methods. Thus, business analysis is the right place to use creativity techniques. Creativity can help in generating content which is later precisely described and analyzed with business models and software models.

2.2 Related Work

Motivation to manage creativity in software company [12] results from continuous changes in market environment and necessity to compete through sustained innovations. Integration of creativity with information systems strategies is a challenge for most organizations.

Creativity in requirements engineering is one of the most popular topics on the edge of creativity and software development. A paper containing literature review [13] maps 46 papers related to creativity and requirements engineering and concludes that "creativity techniques enhance creative thinking in requirements activities" and "creative thinking strategies should be fully integrated in current requirements engineering processes, methods and tools". In order to address the problem that "requirements engineering isn't recognized as a creative process" one can encourage creative thinking during the requirements process with use of theories from cognitive science, e.g. analogical reasoning [14]. An attempt to integrate creativity techniques with different types of use case and system context modeling was made in a scenario-driven requirements engineering process that includes workshops [15]. A remedy in form of combining goal-oriented approach and creativity is proposed for the problem that after creativity workshops "creative outputs are not grounded in user goals, are not amenable to decision support techniques, and cannot be easily captured by non-experts" [16]. A link between business modeling and creativity applied in a business context at a strategic level is made in terms of "a tool which bridges the gap between freedom of actions, encouraging creativity, and constraints, allowing validation and advanced features" [17].

Another popular topic is creativity related to agile projects. A literature review [18] "uses creativity theory as a lens to review the current agile method literature to understand exactly how much we know about the extent to which creativity actually occurs in these agile environments". It reveals many gaps in the body of knowledge and conflicts of opinions in current state as well as issues for further research. eXtreme Programming (XP) has been analyzed and evaluated from the perspective of the creativity, in particular the creative performance and structure required at the teamwork level [19]. Extending an agile process with creativity techniques in a project for a large media organization resulted in better evaluation of requirements by domain experts both in novelty and usefulness categories [20].

Other papers reflect the diversity of topics and issues on the edge of creativity and software development. One can find a review of the literature on measurement of creativity in software products and evaluation of 6 applications with criteria of novelty and utility [21]. In order to facilitate use of creativity techniques which are used as "tools for stimulating creative thinking" [22] authors propose Creativity Patterns Guide tailored for the requirements engineering phase. In category of creative person, preferences of software developers were studied when giving them possibility to spend more time on creative work [23]. An individual-team dynamics in creativity is touched in a framework for enabling software development, interaction design, and information content researchers and managers to understand the opportunities, challenges and principles of social creativity [24]. Regarding the creative environment, an exploratory research has investigated "the role of creative style and climate in work creativity on teams striving to develop innovative IT designs" [25]. It has confirmed a positive relationships between creative style and work creativity, a positive relationship between creative climate stimulants and work creativity, a negative relationship between creative climate obstacles and work creativity, and that creative climate stimulants were significant determinants of work creativity.

There are also reports on applying creativity in education of software developers. Application of "opportunistic software development principles in computer engineering education" allows to produce innovative ideas and solutions by encouraging students to be creative and to develop solutions that cross the boundaries of diverse technologies [26]. Several creativity techniques were applied in education of computer science students [27–29]. A study of an individual creativity-enhancing technique (called Solo-Brainstorming) [30] in area of improving the level of creativity of IT students when identifying requirements in context of software development ends with a recommendation to incorporate creativity-enhancing techniques into the IT course curriculum.

2.3 Creativity Techniques in Software Project

The fundamental assumption underlying stimulating creativity is egalitarian approach to creativity. It is based on research results which reveal that several natural cognitive processes are activated in creative process. They sometimes gain their specifics, such as free use of imagination, outside the box thinking, or flexible categorizations, and they can be stimulated. One of myths about creativity, which was rejected by creativity revisionists, was the belief that creativity is like a sudden illumination. Although some ideas might come suddenly and unexpectedly, usually the creative process is a long-term activity requiring a lot of effort.

In technological applications, one can speak about creative problem solving, which must address both novelty and value (usefulness). Relativity is specific to both these dimensions, what explains the roots of the problems with creativity measurement. There are several types of creativity, including: potential, crystallized, mature and genius creativity. When speaking about creativity in software project, one must address at least the level of mature creativity, which is based on professional knowledge and necessity to meet professional standards of quality. Genius creativity, by definition, happens exceptionally and leads to great discoveries.

Creativity training is a way of stimulating creative processes with expectation that they will be activated later during the work for purpose. Typical creativity trainings are performed as workshops in order to stimulate children's creativity or adult creativity. One of the goals of the training for adults can be formation of creative teams. In this case, a team attends a week-long workshop which consists of morning and afternoon sessions. During each session, 3–5 creativity techniques selected by the trainer are being worked out.

Creativity training handbook [5] collects 134 creativity techniques together with their explanation and examples of topics for elaboration during the sessions. It includes the following groups of techniques:

- Interpersonal skills - which aim at creating team spirit and removing obstacles for interpersonal communication and cooperation,
- Creativity skills - which include skills of abstract thinking, making associations, deduction, induction (analogy), use of metaphors, and transformation of the knowledge,
- Motivation - which can be based on motive catalogues, on increase of interests as well as on discovery of negative aspects to be repaired,
- Overcoming obstacles to creativity and acquiring new creativity patterns - which appear to be important part of every training.

Several issues appear when trying to apply creativity techniques in software-related area. Their root lies in the difference between the context of their discovery together with their typical application for creativity training and the context of application in software project. One can notice that one of the reasons why they are not used is the fact, that software engineers do not know them. So, the question is, having such a big number of techniques, which of them are the most useful for achieving project's objectives?

Assuming that software engineers know creativity techniques, does it mean that they can apply them properly? Sometimes creativity trainings are organized for students of computer science. But what is their impact on software project (long time after the training)? The impact of creativity training on software project has not been studied extensively so far.

Additionally, one can ask question whether they can be applied not only as tools for creativity training but also directing creativity? As creativity in software process is related not only to generation of ideas but also preparation, elaboration of consistent solution and validation - which techniques can support given micro-dimensions of creative process?

3   Quasi-experiment with Training-Application-Feedback Cycle

In theory, a big number of creativity techniques can be applied in software project for both creativity training and directing creativity. But, how it is in practice? This quasi-experiment aims at exploring this issue. The following sub-sections present:

- an overview of the quasi-experiment,
- the Training-Application-Feedback cycle,
- creativity techniques selected for explorations together with examples of topics for training and for application in software related context,
- a questionnaire for collecting feedback data,
- comments on the conduct of the empirical studies,
- and remarks on research method.

3.1 Overview

Figure 1 presents an overview of the quasi-experiment.

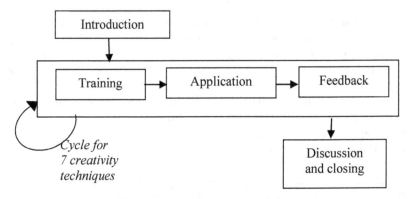

Fig. 1. Parts of the quasi-experiment

The quasi-experiment started with an introduction. It included a brief presentation of creativity in arts and creative problem solving in technology, kinds of creativity, and impact of creativity techniques on the software project. The goals of the experiment and its rules were explained and participants have filled out initial part of the questionnaire. Then, Training-Application-Feedback cycle (described in details in the Subsect. 3.2) was performed for 7 creativity techniques (described in details in the Subsect. 3.3). Participants were evaluating ease of use, level of interest and usefulness. They were also writing down any comments related to a given creativity technique (see details in Subsect. 3.4). Finally, the part of closing and discussion was performed. The participants filled out closing part of the questionnaire and they could share their reflections from participation in the experiment and confront them with the opinions of other participants. It is important to mention that they handed only the questionnaires (keeping results of their creative work for themselves) and they were encouraged to share their reflections to the extent they felt comfortable.

3.2 Activities in Training-Application-Feedback Cycle

The parts of the Training-Application-Feedback cycle address important problems related to application of creativity techniques in software project, i.e. first - creativity techniques are not used because software engineers don't know them, and the second - software engineers have gone through creativity training but they don't know how to apply the techniques in software project. The training is related with the first problem, the application part - with the second. The feedback is collected for research purpose.

The training part started with a short explanation of the creativity technique by the experimenter including information about the goal of applying a given technique and background mechanisms as well as activities to be performed. After this explanation, training in form of a short exercise (approximately 5 min) was made to learn by doing this technique with topics used in general creativity trainings.

The application part dealt with the application of newly-learned creativity technique for elaboration of software-related problems (approximately 10 min). A flexible approach to selecting problems at hand for this part was taken in order to achieve participant's involvement. Thus, the problem could be related to research, software project, thesis in case of diploma students, innovation made by software systems or any solution in the area related to software. The participants were encouraged to think about issues they work on and to do it in such a way which allows to achieve as many benefits from participation in this experiments as they can. They were asked to write the results of their work down, but they didn't have to show them to anyone later. This respect to privacy was necessary in order to ensure comfort of the participants, especially in situations in which they wouldn't like to share their ideas for innovative solutions with other participants or they might want to hide their obstacles in creativity. In case of techniques related to overcoming obstacles (See Subsect. 3.3: *I could be more creative if...*; and *Let's invite him/her...*) there was just one joint part instead of training and application parts.

The feedback was collected with a questionnaire they were filling out for a given creativity technique after application part. It included evaluation of the techniques in the following dimensions: easy-difficult, interesting-boring and useful-useless. They were encouraged to share as many comments as possible.

3.3 Creativity Techniques Under Exploration

Seven creativity techniques from three groups of techniques were selected for exploration. These were:

- *Naive questions* and *Reverse brainstorming* from the Motivations group,
- *Lunette*, *Chinese dictionary* and *What if...* from the Skills group,
- *I could be more creative if...* and *Let's invite her/him...* from the Obstacle overcoming group.

Naive questions aim at increasing motivation through discovery of values, hidden assumptions, implicit knowledge, and other aspects which seem to be obvious although they are not. It allows to better understand the essence of the problem and to propose the right change. The exercise starts with an introduction to the context: "Imagine a child or an alien… Someone who doesn't understand basics of civilized world and he/she asks naive, unexpected questions. And after receiving an answer, he/she asks the next question…" (It's task for 2 persons.) During the training, participants have used the topic: Why do people work? In the application phase, they were trying to answer the following questions: Why the topic of your project is important? Why it is worth doing?

Reverse brainstorming deals with expression of overwhelming negativism and criticism. It is based on the internal tendency to repair and improve. In other words, exposing people to negative aspects should motivate them to positive actions. The task in the exercise was to identify all possible defects, weaknesses and other annoying things. During the training, we started with a question: what don't you like… in your town? At the university? In drivers' behaviors? In application phase, participants were working with one of the following questions: What don't you like in a given area (in order to propose a change)? What don't you like in solutions of others (in order to find a space for your contribution)? What don't you like in your solution (in order to eliminate defects and improve it)?

Lunette is the first technique from the skills group. It allows to see reality (or artifacts) at different levels of abstraction with relationships among the views representing overview of entire object and richness of details. It uses typical generalization-specialization skills (or top-down and bottom-up approaches) and it leads to novel discoveries via untypical views or details other haven't seen. It can be also used as a way for systematic generation of descriptions. During the training, the participants used this technique for description of their past or future holidays or their hobbies. They were instructed to move between levels of abstraction and to discover something new. In the phase of application, they were encouraged to start with describing their project or solution in one sentence and then consciously focus on several issues, parts, pieces of evidence etc.

Chinese dictionary technique performance started with presentation of an old animal taxonomy (totally different from contemporary taxonomies). This technique encourages to creating untypical classifications. Such classifications which are useful for us. During the training, the participants could create their own classification of animals, or types of activities…, or products in the market… In the phase of application to software project, participants were creating their own taxonomies of issues related to project, tasks in the projects or other software-related artifacts.

What if… is an exercise for searching hidden sequences of consequences. It is based on remote associations in human mind. The discovery of possible consequences might lead to new opportunities or outside the box solutions. During the training, the following topics were used: What if… gravity law did not work anymore? What if… shoes got alive? In the phase of application in software-related context, the participants were considering consequences of application of their research results, systems or solutions. What if… someone applied them in a given context? What if… all must have used this approach, system or solution?

I could be more creative if… is a technique for increasing understanding of personal obstacles to creativity which should be helpful in overcoming them later. The task for participants was to complete this sentence with 7 ideas. They were informed that people usually start with external conditions which they cannot change, but it is good to consider also personal aspects which we can influence.

Let's invite him/her... is about using creativity patterns of experts in creativity. The participants were encouraged to think and choose their symbol of creativity (an expert in creativity). Is it any scientist? An artist? A leader of famous IT business? A science-fiction creature? A multi-millionaire? Then, they should have imagined (variant 1) that we invited him/her and asked for advices how to be more creative... What they could say? Or, they should have imagined (variant 2) how the creativity expert dealt with their projects. What would they have done? What kind of attitude would they have taken? During this task for imagination, they should list at least 7 ideas of successful creativity patterns.

3.4 Questionnaire

The initial part of the questionnaire collected the following information:

- assessment of participant's potential creativity in scale of 0–10 (0-very low - 10 very high),
- assessment of participant's actual creativity level in scale of 0–10 (0-very low - 10 very high),
- evaluation of participant's need for creativity training in scale of 0–10 (0-very low - 10 very high),
- Earlier participation in creativity training (yes/no).

Each technique was evaluated in 3-dimensional scale:

- dimension 1: easy - rather easy - rather difficult - difficult,
- dimension 2: interesting - rather interesting - rather boring - boring,
- dimension 3: useful - rather useful - rather useless - useless

Participants were encouraged to add as many comments as possible. Three-dimensional evaluation was made in order to gain a common ground for comparisons. The evaluation in the scale and comments were expected to collect opinions of participants about the application of creativity techniques.

Final part of the questionnaire was related to the results of training and it contained the following questions:

- Was it helpful in increasing your creativity? (answers in scale: yes - rather yes - rather no - no),
- Was it helpful in understanding what creativity is about? (answers in scale: yes - rather yes - rather no - no),
- Are you going to use creativity techniques in future? (answers in scale: yes - rather yes - rather no - no),
- Why?

3.5   Comments on Conduct

The following participants took part in the experiment:

- Six persons of academic staff who perform their teaching and research in software related area,
- Five diploma students who work on their Bachelor or Master thesis in the area of software engineering,
- One person working in social sciences who represented a perspective of personal development.

There were 6 women and 6 men. The participants spent about 1.5–2.5 h on experiment. All of them assessed higher potential creativity than actual one. They haven't participated in creativity training before and they expressed diversified need of creativity training (2–10).

The academic staff can be characterized by diversity of expertise and personality. Their expertise ranged over business analysis, programming, IT technologies, software engineering, social aspects of IT, and business aspects of IT technologies. This group included both individuals with an open, positive attitude as well as very critical persons. This personality specifics can be seen in all answers they were giving. It is worth to mention that some of them really tried to be objective and they were describing both positive and negative aspects of creativity techniques in their comments. To sum up, this diversity of participants allow to expect that they are a good sample to cover possible diversity of opinions about application of creativity techniques.

3.6   Remarks on Research Method

The problem with research on creativity in software development, and especially the use of creativity techniques in software project, is in broad scope of inter-related issues and variables. It is not possible to answer completely any research question in one study. Applying approach of craft of research [31], the research questions (in introduction and following discussion) represent what we would like to know about use of creativity techniques in software project, and the goals of study take into account limited capability of the study. The results contribute to answering research questions, but they don't give complete answers.

Quasi-experiment [32] is applied as a research method when effects of some treatments are measured or observed, but researchers don't have control over all variables. They are applied typically in context of scarcity of data, e.g. state of patient after a treatment in medicine. In this case, it is even more complex, because the topic of research is related with the phenomena to be constructed. Participants, who do not know techniques or use them unconsciously, could not properly report on their use. Thus, the design of these studies includes giving the experience (construct a new phenomena) which is equivalent to treatment. A straight application of creativity techniques in software-related area would most likely suffer from problems related to trial-and-error phenomena which appear when people learn something new. The training alone would not make a proper experience of applying them to software development. Thus, the treatment aimed at creation of participant's mindset able to provide valid data must have two parts: training in a simple domain and when participants have felt comfortable with a given creativity technique - application in software-related context.

Design of the feedback part has applied principia of exploratory studies and use of mixed qualitative and quantitative approaches [33]. The exploratory focus was on possibility of application and its specifics expressed in comments. A realistic flexibility of applications was allowed and qualitative data play the primary role. The opinions whether a technique is easy, interesting and useful are quantified in order to make some comparisons between the techniques.

4   Research Results and Their Interpretation

The research results for all creativity techniques are presented in the following sub-sections. They include presentation of opinions about the techniques for both academics (6 academic staff in software related area and 1 researcher in social sciences) and 5 diploma students. Positive value answers (easy, interesting, useful) were assigned with weight equal to 2; rather positive (rather easy, rather interesting, rather useful) - weight equal to 1; rather negative (rather difficult, rather boring, rather useless) - weight equal to -1; and negative (difficult, boring, useless) - weight equal to -2. The average value (av.) is calculated as a weighted sum of all answers divided by the number of participants in the group. The summary of comments contains presentation of both positive and negative opinions. It covers also information about difficulties encountered by participants and other information specific for a given technique.

4.1   Results for *Naive Questions*

Table 1 presents opinions about *naive questions*. The differences between the groups are rather small. This technique was viewed in a very positive way.

Table 1. Opinions about *naive questions*

Academic staff					av.	Diploma students					av.
Easy	3	4		Difficult	1.43	Easy	5			Difficult	2
Interest.	2	4	1	Boring	1	Interest.	2	3		Boring	1.4
Useful	4	2	1	Useless	1.29	Useful	1	4		Useless	1.2

A few participants have appreciated that it allows to question things that seem obvious and think again about their sense. It allows to reach original ideas, goals, needs... the essence. It helps to clear mind from typical ways of thinking which are based on learned knowledge or everyday experience. It allows to reject myths. It can be useful in problem analysis and making decision in projects. In fact, when some participants got to the non-conscious level, they have realized that the questions are not naive anymore. The participants noticed that "asking questions is easy, but answering them - is not". The most popular difficulty was "when to stop asking new questions". A critical participant said that he was using this technique without awareness and it shouldn't be called a technique. (He had the same opinion about the next technique.) Another participant, who admitted "he didn't go deep", said that he was previously aware of all the results of this exercise.

4.2 Results for *Reverse Brainstorming*

Table 2 presents opinions about *Reverse brainstorming*. This technique was the most controversial. The differences in average opinions are 0.8 or bigger in all dimensions. Additionally, there were several differences in its perception by participants in the same group.

Table 2. Opinions about *Reverse brainstorming*

Academic staff					av.	Diploma students					av.
Easy	2	2	3	Difficult	0.43	Easy	4	1		Difficult	1.8
Interest.	3	3	1	Boring	1.14	Interest.	2		3	Boring	0.2
Useful	4	1	2	Useless	1	Useful	2		3	Useless	0.2

Positive comments have shown a lot of enthusiasm towards this technique, e.g. "the best of all techniques", "it allows to identify problems explicitly", "starting from negativism is easier", "very easy to find defects, and then we know what to improve", "it allows to overcome barriers to expressing criticism". One of critical comments suggested a possible opposite effect, i.e. "With too much of criticism, motivation to discovery might decrease. It's rather discouraging." Others have noticed that criticism is often right, but it doesn't solve problems. The attitude to this technique strongly depends on personality. Some participants admitted they felt resistance to express criticism. Others didn't like negative perspective, e.g. "this is not a technique for optimistic people". Yet others claimed that they didn't need to practice it, because critical way of thinking was typical for them.

4.3 Results for *Lunette*

Table 3 presents opinions about *Lunette*. The difference in average opinions only in case of usefulness is bigger than 0.6. Although average results show rather positive perception, this technique was probably the most challenging.

Some participants have found the value of this technique in conscious and systematic approach which allows for building consistent representation, e.g. "a new approach which requires focusing on issues", "it allows to understand problem better by focusing in several dimensions". For one of them, it would be helpful to add representation of levels of details. However, they have shared a lot of difficulties, e.g. a difficulty to select what to focus on, a difficulty to focus on unknown details, a difficulty to "change direction" after

Table 3. Opinions about *Lunette*

Academic staff						av.	Diploma students						av.
Easy	2	3	1	1	Difficult	0.57	Easy	1	2	2		Difficult	0.4
Interest.	2	3	2		Boring	0.71	Interest.		4	1		Boring	0.6
Useful	3	2	2		Useless	0.86	Useful			3	2	Useless	0.2

work on details, and a difficulty to switch between content and managing this content. The most critical participant doubted about its impact on creativity (and he expressed the same for two following techniques as well.). Another critical participant wondered about possibilities of applying this technique in software development process and he expected a more clear clue where to use it.

4.4 Results for *Chinese Dictionary*

Table 4 presents opinions about *Chinese dictionary*. The differences in average opinions about ease of use and level of interest are quite high: 0.93 and 1.29 respectively. This technique was the most interesting for diploma students as it supported "outside the box" thinking.

Table 4. Opinions about *Chinese dictionary*

Academic staff						av.	Diploma students					av.
Easy	4	3			Difficult	1.57	Easy	2	1	2	Difficult	0.6
Interest.	2	3	2		Boring	0.71	Interest.	5			Boring	2
Useful	3	2		2	Useless	0.57	Useful	3	1	1	Useless	1

In software engineering area, we are used to precise taxonomies. At first, this technique encountered astonishment, feeling of a chaotic approach and feeling of difficulty in some cases. Then, some participants appreciated its usefulness for broadening their perspective, thinking outside the box, discovering new dimensions for already known topic, and prioritetization in the project. It has appeared that this is a typical approach in social sciences. The critical participants couldn't see any benefits from untypical classifications till the end of cycle. One of them indicated for technological constraints as a reason of their problematic use.

4.5 Results for *What if*

Table 5 presents opinions about *What if...* It can be called the most rational creativity technique.

The participant who had the expertise in business analysis noticed that this is a fundamental method of dealing with multi-dimensional complexity. It allows for making

Table 5. Opinions about *What if...*

Academic staff						av.	Diploma students					av.
Easy	2	3	1	1	Difficult	0.57	Easy	1	3	1	Difficult	0.8
Interest.	3	3	1		Boring	1.14	Interest.	1	3	1	Boring	0.8
Useful	4		2	1	Useless	0.57	Useful	2	2	1	Useless	1

decisions regarding the business process based on analysis results. Other participants discovered new possibilities, user experience issues, or new functionalities. For others, it allowed to check what happens in case of unexpected consequences. It appeared to be useful for predicting all consequences including threats to failure of the project. The difficulties had several sources. As one of the participants said "just performing this exercise in a creative way is difficult to persons with rational minds". Even more difficult was to reach final conclusion. Others reported difficulties related to interpretation of long sequences of consequences and taking responsibility for them or reaching conclusions which are hard to be accepted. The most critical participant stated that he didn't see any application of this technique in research and at this point he was more and more disappointed with creativity techniques.

4.6 Results for *I could be more creative*

Table 6 presents opinions about *I could be more creative...* The difference in average opinions is big in case of ease of use and usefulness, 0.89 and 0.69 respectively. This technique was considered as useful for long-term personal development.

Table 6. Opinions about *I could be more...*

Academic staff						av.	Diploma students					av.
Easy	4	2	1		Difficult	1.29	Easy	1	2	2	Difficult	0.4
Interest.	3	3	1		Boring	1.14	Interest.	3	2		Boring	1.6
Useful	3	2	1	1	Useless	0.71	Useful	2	3		Useless	1.4

The participants have reported a lot of positive comments, e.g. "it helps to find obstacles to creativity and encourages to make brave decisions", or "discovery!". They noticed that only honest answer to this question allows to identify real reasons and that "it's not easy to accept findings about your own weaknesses". However, "it is useful in a broader sense, i.e. for long-term personal development". The fact of becoming aware of the obstacles somehow makes them weaker. One can undertake actions in order to overcome them. The participant with expertise in management claimed that "this technique is a good self-justifications, creativity doesn't depend on circumstances". The critical participants complained that identification of obstacles to creativity does not directly help in eliminating them.

4.7 Results for *Let's invite him/her*

Table 7 presents opinions about *Let's invite him/her...* This technique was the most difficult for participants.

Table 7. Opinions about *Let's invite him/her...*

Academic staff					av.	Diploma students					av.
Easy	1	2	3	1	Difficult	−0.14	Easy	1	1	3		Difficult	0
Interest.	4	1	2		Boring	1	Interest.	2	2		1	Boring	0.8
Useful	1	4	1	1	Useless	0.43	Useful	2	1	2		Useless	0.6

Positive comments were associated with discovering interesting attitudes, e.g. positive attitude, hard work, strength in fighting against all kinds of problems, or for taking the approach which has lead someone to success in IT area. The results of this exercise depended on "who is invited" and whether participants really have known their experts in creativity. Anyway, they could bring "several benefits to our project." The participants have reported difficulties with imagination of creative persons and situation of inviting him or her. The most critical participant has expressed it in the following way: "How can I know what this creativity symbol might think???".

4.8 Results of Closing Part

A majority of the participants were leaving the experiment with some increase of creativity, better understanding of what creativity is about and a rather positive attitude to using creativity techniques in future. Final remarks included positive comments, e.g. "Some of them are really interesting", "the experiment helped to understand creativity in a non-trivial way". A few participants appreciated values coming from all three groups of creativity techniques, i.e. increase in motivation, more awareness regarding skills needed for creativity, and the ways of dealing with obstacles. In their opinion, "a mix of creativity techniques will be useful in practice." But they agreed that in order to use selected creativity techniques they must know them. They felt encouraged to spend more time on development of their creativity skills. The most critical participant concluded that he cannot see usefulness of these creativity techniques for scientific research. He wrote: "It seems to me that these techniques might be useful for stimulating creativity of young children." The second critical participant admitted that, in his opinion, creativity is like an insight. This was contradictory to methodological approach, but "some of the techniques might be useful in some cases."

4.9 Analysis of Threats to Validity

The research results should be interpreted in categories of exploratory research. So far, creativity trainings were applied by presumption of positive effects on participants without evidence that they really work. This research was an attempt to check it in a methodological way. Obviously, it was not free from constraints and threats to validity. First of all, we have selected just 7 from about 150 creativity techniques for the experiment. Second, 12 participants are a small sample of thousands of potential users of creativity techniques in software related context. These factors should be taken into account when making interpretation and generalization. Having said this, let's analyze validity issues in details.

The following aspects of study aimed at assuring theory validity. Creativity techniques have been taken from the handbook written by creativity researchers. Thus, there should be no mistake related to the content of creativity techniques. The difference between context of discovery of these techniques and the context of application in software related area was addressed during the quasi-experiment design by splitting the part of training from the part of application. Selected creativity techniques were taken from different groups in order to represent the diversity of creativity techniques.

In order to assure experiment validity, we have addressed two main problems related to application of creativity techniques in software related context. The participants have gone through training in order to learn the techniques, and they were encouraged to apply them to software-related problems, which required creativity and were interesting for them. The experimenter took care about potential benefits, comfort and personal privacy of the participants.

The number of techniques under exploration was a compromise between the desire to cover large number of techniques and realistic planning of comfortable work and reliable results. In order to assure data collection validity (including participants validity and elimination of researcher bias), the following actions have been undertaken. In the design phase, the decision was to collect both opinions in scale and comments. The data in scale allow to compare opinions about the techniques in three dimensions. The comments allow to discover more details and to broaden perspective.

The precision of participant's opinions is not very high. Their opinions about use of creativity techniques might change in future. Together with the fact that there were only 12 participants, we decided not to use advanced statistics methods to avoid impression of precision which is not delivered. In fact, honest and extensive comments are much more valuable. The experiment was conducted in Polish, thus some threats to validity might result from translations of the comments. In order to minimize this risk, we focused on meaning rather than on literal expressions during the translation.

In order to eliminate researcher's bias, it was clearly announced at the beginning that we are interested "to see reality as it is" and not to prove anything. The participants were a small sample of all possible users of creativity techniques, but the fact that they were a very diversified group with respect to age, gender, experience and attitude allows to expect that threats to participants validity were minimized.

4.10 Interpretation and Issues for Further Studies

This study doesn't allow to give complete answers to all research questions. Instead, it allows to see the diversity of aspects and issues which should be taken into account in further studies. All creativity techniques (with just one exception) gained on average positive opinions in all three dimensions. Although none of participants made a great discovery during the experiment, most of them are going to use creativity techniques in future. Thus, their usefulness in generating innovation is promising.

Naive questions gained the best opinions, i.e. 1.2 or more on average in each group and each dimension. However, these opinions are not supported by any evidence that it has led to any discovery. Quite often, the same technique received contradictory feedback both in one group and in dimension of students vs. academics. Thus, it doesn't allow us to recommended any of them more than others for the use in software related context. It can only encourage us for searching for factors on which it depends.

One of such factors is users' attitude. These participants who were involved, gained a more interesting results. They have got a broader perspective. They could even discover that naive question are not naive indeed. On the other hand, those who doubted, lost their chance to become more conscious about nature of creativity processes and to overcome their obstacles to creativity. It is good to remind that creativity techniques are usually at lower level of abstraction than software engineering techniques. They support certain cognitive processes which should be consciously used for both organizing and performing creative tasks.

The perception of creativity techniques depends also on personality and previous experience. The personality specifics appeared the most clearly in confrontation with criticism (reverse brainstorming technique). For some participants, it was the best technique, while for others - it could "cause the opposite effect". When a given style of thinking is natural for someone there is no need to teach him this style. A given style can be natural due to performing some kind of activities, e.g. *what if...* by the business analyst or untypical classifications (*Chinese dictionary*) by the researcher in social sciences.

What they are good for? Let's take perspective of micro-dimensions of creative process, i.e. preparation, idea generation, elaboration of consistent vision and validation. The techniques of *naive questions* and *reverse brainstorming* can be helpful in preparation. *Chinese dictionary* can support idea generation. *Lunette* can be useful in elaboration of consistent vision of solution. *What if...* technique can find its application in validation of vision. They play a supportive role. None can guarantee that the product will be original. Two last techniques, i.e. *I could be creative if...* and *Let's invite him/her...* rather do not have application for directing creativity in software project. They are useful just for training creativity skills.

An interesting issue is in interplay between rationality and creativity. Is the way to success in their smooth interplay? Is it in broadening perspective and including aspects which others couldn't associate or integrate? Another interesting issue is related to the fact, that several creativity techniques appeal to imagination when setting context, e.g. "imagine a child or an alien..." Could we get rid of them? Could we ask just rational questions instead? This study doesn't give insights in this area although they seem to be important. In dynamic situations where adaptation to the actual needs and existing skills in the team is required, project managers can undertake management of processes related to creativity training and directing creativity with selected techniques. The fact that the participants of the study have easily learned the techniques and for most of them these techniques were interesting, seem to be a promising sign for conducting similar sessions in real software projects.

5 Conclusions

This research aimed at exploring application of creativity techniques in software-related context. Creativity research and the creativity training handbook were used as fundamentals for this research. Seven creativity techniques from different groups of creativity techniques were selected, which allowed to have a diversified sample of techniques. General observation for all creativity techniques is that they are at lower level of abstraction comparing to software engineering techniques. They often address a specific aspect of creativity process. Thus, they do not replace software engineering techniques. When applied in a proper way, they can support (but not guarantee!) creativity process in software project.

The quasi-experiment was conducted in training-application-feedback cycle. The contribution of this research is the feedback on the creativity techniques after not only creativity training but also their application in software-related context. The study has shown that the following issues have impact on applicability:

- A technique itself and its potential use in a given stage of creativity process,
- Familiarity of participants with creativity techniques,
- Positive attitude towards applying them in software project,
- Personality and previous experience of the user,
- Aspects related to interplay between rationality and creativity,
- Objectives of application, i.e. whether it is used in creativity training (for switching on a certain kind of thinking and behaviors, learning how to overcome obstacles) or it is used for directing creativity in a given project.

Regarding recommendations for practice which result from the studies, we can say that it is a question of awareness of issues related to creativity and skills for their proper application. Project managers who are interested in increasing creativity and innovation should manage creativity issues in teams and projects. As many factors have impact on results, the best practice is to keep trying the most promising creativity techniques and analyze their impact on project. For more precise recommendations regarding usefulness of creativity techniques in further work, one can analyze creativity mechanisms and context of discovery of creativity techniques. The method of performing empirical studies in Training-Application-Feedback cycle appeared to be a useful tool in exploring applicability of creativity techniques in software related context and it can be recommended to further empirical studies with other creativity techniques.

Acknowledgements. I wish to thank all participants of the quasi-experiment for their honest and extensive opinions.

References

1. VanGundy, A.B.: 101 Activities for Teaching Creativity and Problem Solving. Pfeiffer, A Wiley Imprint (2005)
2. de Bono, E.: Serious Creativity. HarperCollins Publishing, New York (1992)

3. Higgins, J.M.: 101 Creative Problem Solving Techniques. New Management Publishing Company, Winter Park, FL (1994)
4. von Oech, R.: A Whack on the Side of the Head. Warner Books, New York (2008)
5. Nęcka, E., Orzechowski, J., Słabosz, A., Szymura, B.: Trening twórczości (Creativity training). Gdańskie Wydawnictwo Psychologiczne (2013)
6. Nęcka, E.: Psychologia twórczości (Creativity psychology). Gdańskie Wydawnictwo Psychologiczne (2012)
7. Plsek, P.E.: Creativity, Innovation, and Quality. ASQC Quality Press, Milwaukee (1997)
8. Bobkowska, A.: Balance between creativity and methodology in software project. In: Proceedings of the 2015 Mutlimedia, Interaction, Design and Innovation International Conference (MIDI 2015). ACM Press (2015) https://doi.org/10.1145/2814464.2814468
9. Bobkowska, A.: Zarządzanie kreatywnością w projekcie (Creativity Management in Projects). Res. Enterp. Mod. Econ. Theory Pract. 21 (2017). https://doi.org/10.19253/reme.2017.02.002
10. Bobkowska, A.: Ryzyko kreatywności w projektach informatycznych (Creativity Risk in Software Projects). Res. Enterp. Mod. Econ. Theory Pract. 26 (2018). https://doi.org/10.19253/reme.2018.03.003
11. Bobkowska, A.: Positive risk of creativity in software projects: an expected result, a threat or an opportunity? In: 11th International Conference on Human System Interaction (HSI) (2018). https://doi.org/10.1109/hsi.2018.8431364
12. Ulrich, F., Mengiste, S.A.: The challenges of creativity in software organizations. In: Bergvall-Kåreborn, B., Nielsen, P.A. (eds.) TDIT 2014. IFIPAICT, vol. 429, pp. 16–34. Springer, Heidelberg (2014). https://doi.org/10.1007/978-3-662-43459-8_2
13. Lemos, J., Alves, C., Duboc, L., Rodrigues, G.N.: A systematic mapping study on creativity in requirements engineering. In: Proceedings of the 27th Annual ACM Symposium on Applied Computing (SAC 2012). ACM, New York (2012). https://doi.org/10.1145/2245276.2231945
14. Maiden, N., Gizikis, A., Robertson, S.: Provoking creativity: imagine what your requirements could be like. IEEE Softw. 21, 68–75 (2004)
15. Maiden, N., Manning, S., Robertson, S., Greenwood, J.: Integrating creativity workshops into structured requirements processes. In: Proceedings of the 5th Conference on Designing Interactive Systems: Processes, Practices, Methods, and Techniques (DIS 2004). ACM, New York (2004). https://doi.org/10.1145/1013115.1013132
16. Horkoff, J., Maiden, N., Lockerbie, J.: Creativity and goal modeling for software requirements engineering. In: Proceedings of the 2015 ACM SIGCHI Conference on Creativity and Cognition (C&C 2015). ACM, New York (2015). https://doi.org/10.1145/2757226.2764544
17. Fritscher, B., Pigneur, Y.: Supporting business model modelling: a compromise between creativity and constraints. In: England, D., Palanque, P., Vanderdonckt, J., Wild, Peter J. (eds.) TAMODIA 2009. LNCS, vol. 5963, pp. 28–43. Springer, Heidelberg (2010). https://doi.org/10.1007/978-3-642-11797-8_3
18. Conboy, K., Wang, X., Fitzgerald, B.: Creativity in agile systems development: a literature review. In: Dhillon, G., Stahl, B.C., Baskerville, R. (eds.) CreativeSME 2009. IFIPAICT, vol. 301, pp. 122–304. Springer, Heidelberg (2009). https://doi.org/10.1007/978-3-642-02388-0_9
19. de la Barra, C.L., Crawford, B.: Fostering creativity thinking in agile software development. In: Holzinger, A. (ed.) USAB 2007. LNCS, vol. 4799, pp. 415–426. Springer, Heidelberg (2007). https://doi.org/10.1007/978-3-540-76805-0_37
20. Hollis, B., Maiden, N.: Extending agile processes with creativity techniques. IEEE Softw. 30, 78–84 (2013)
21. Couger, J.D., Dengate, G.: Measurement of creativity of IS products. In: Proceedings of the Twenty-Fifth Hawaii International Conference on System Sciences (1992)

22. Vieira, Elton R., Alves, C., Duboc, L.: Creativity Patterns Guide: Support for the Application of Creativity Techniques in Requirements Engineering. In: Winckler, M., Forbrig, P., Bernhaupt, R. (eds.) HCSE 2012. LNCS, vol. 7623, pp. 283–290. Springer, Heidelberg (2012). https://doi.org/10.1007/978-3-642-34347-6_19

23. Gu, M., Tong, X.: Towards Hypotheses on Creativity in Software Development. In: Bomarius, F., Iida, H. (eds.) PROFES 2004. LNCS, vol. 3009, pp. 47–61. Springer, Heidelberg (2004). https://doi.org/10.1007/978-3-540-24659-6_4

24. Fischer, G., Giaccardi, E.: Sustaining social creativity. Commun. ACM **50**, 12 (2007)

25. Fagan, M.H.: The influence of creative style and climate on software development team creativity: an exporatory study. J. Comput. Inf. Syst. **44**, 3 (2004)

26. Obrenovic, Z., Gaševic, D., Eliëns, A.: Stimulating creativity through opportunistic software development. IEEE Softw. **25**, 64–70 (2008)

27. Knobelsdorf, M., Romeike, R.: Creativity as a pathway to computer science. In: Proceedings of ITiCSE 2008. ACM Press (2008). https://doi.org/10.1145/1597849.1384347

28. Salgian, A., Ault, Ch., Nakra, T.M., Wang, Y.: Teaching creativity in computer science. In: Proceedings SIGCSE 2013. ACM Press (2013)

29. Kwasnik, M.: Nature of creativity in computer science education. designing innovative workshops for CS students. In: Proceedings of the 2014 Multimedia, Interaction, Design and Innovation International Conference (MIDI 2014). ACM Press (2014). https://doi.org/10.1145/2643572.2643580

30. Aurum, A., Handzic, M., Gardiner, A.: Supporting creativity in software development: an application in IT education. In: Tomei, L. (ed.) Online and Distance Learning: Concepts, Methodologies, Tools, and Applications. IGI Global, Hershey (2008)

31. Booth, W.C., Colomb, G.G., Williams, J.M.: The Craft of Research, 3rd edn. University of Chicago Press, Chicago (2008)

32. Campbell, D.T., Stanley, J.C.: Experimental and Quasi-experimental Designs for Research. Houghton Mifflin Company, Boston (1963)

33. Creswell, J.W., Plano-Clark, V.L.: Designing and Conducting Mixed Methods Research. SAGE Publications, Thousand Oaks (2010)

Formal Methods

SHACL Shapes Generation from Textual Documents

David Šenkýř[(✉)]

Faculty of Information Technology, Czech Technical University in Prague,
Prague, Czech Republic
`david.senkyr@fit.cvut.cz`

Abstract. *Shapes Constraint Language* (SHACL) is the new recommendation by W3C consortium to uniform both describing and constraining the content of an *RDF graph*. Based on the inspiration of model generation from textual requirements specifications, we investigate the possibility of mapping parts of a textual document to *shapes* described by SHACL. In this contribution, we present our approach of the *patterns* (based on a *grammatical inspection*) that indicates candidates of domain description in SHACL language. We argue that the standard methods of linguistics can be supported by ontology resources as *Schema.org*.

Keywords: SHACL · Text processing · Grammatical inspection · Patterns · Ontology · RDF · OWL

1 Introduction

The problem of model generation based on textual requirements specification is still a popular topic of research, as it proves by [2,4,10] and also our paper [16]. The traditional output of model generation is in the form of *UML diagrams* (typically *class diagram*) that represent a mapping of the problem domain (a part of reality) into the model. This discipline is called *conceptual modelling* [13].

Computerized processing of natural language can be supported by acquired semantic knowledge from an appropriate corresponding *ontology database*. It may be difficult to obtain the ontology related to the client's domain – for many sectors, such ontology is not available. On the other hand, ontology databases for common language are available, e.g., WordNET, ConceptNet, DBpedia, Freebase, OpenCyc.

Nowadays, we can use *Web Ontology Language* (OWL) W3C consortium recommendation or the new one recommendation called *Shapes Constraint Language* (SHACL). Inspired by the ontology-based approach, we decided to apply methods of computerized natural language processing together with data provided by an existing ontology database to generate SHACL expressions. In this contribution, we do not focus only on textual requirements specifications, but we consider the arbitrary textual document as an input source.

© Springer Nature Switzerland AG 2019
R. Pergl et al. (Eds.): EOMAS 2019, LNBIP 366, pp. 121–130, 2019.
https://doi.org/10.1007/978-3-030-35646-0_9

Following the outlined motivation, we have focused our research on two topics. How to extract the knowledge from the plain text in the form of SHACL shapes? Also, how to complete these shapes with some ontology resource?

This paper is divided into two parts. In the first section, we introduce the domain. In the second section, we illustrate our approach of patterns and usage of the ontology database, together with an example of the generated result.

2   Related Work and Terminology

In this section, we introduce the domains and the basic terminology that we face in this paper.

2.1   Conceptual Modelling and Ontologies

Professor Mylopoulos in his paper [13] defined *conceptual modelling* as *"the activity of formally describing some aspects of the physical and social world around us for purposes of understanding and communication"*. The understanding is typically the key factor of a successful product as a result of conceptual modelling. Therefore, we should eliminate the defects of ambiguity, inconsistency, and incompleteness.

In that case, we can be supported by ontologies. In the context of information technologies, the ontology represents knowledge in the form of entities (concepts), properties, and relations between them using a formal encoding. In the first point of view, the ontology should assist with the term definitions, and in the second point of view, it should also help with the detection of some constraint violation. Also, the study [21] shows that it is better to use ontology-driven languages (such as OntoUML) over traditional approaches with UML or E-R models.

2.2   Structured Knowledge on Web

Most, but not all of the structured knowledge on the Web is deeply connected to the *Semantic Web* and its standards. From history, we can mention the original intention of HTML *meta tags*, which were unfortunately predominantly used for spam – therefore, they are widely ignored by search engines [18].

Nowadays, we can use description-logic-based languages (e.g., OWL, Shacl) provided in the form of a recommendation by W3C consortium. Based on them, in the second half of the 2000s, projects like *DBpedia*[1] [3], *Freebase*[2], or *Schema.org*[3] started. They represent *knowledge graphs* (ontologies) formed by RDF *triplets*. We can also mention a semantic network called *ConceptNet*[4] [17]

---

[1] https://wiki.dbpedia.org/.
[2] Terminated project – data still available via https://developers.google.com/freebase.
[3] https://schema.org.
[4] http://www.conceptnet.io.

that combines its own data with other resources (including mentioned *DBpedia*) to provide meanings of word or phrase entered as a query.

Let us briefly introduce the mentioned standards and corresponding technologies.

RDF. The *Resource Description Framework* (RDF) [5] is W3C specification used as a general approach for conceptual modelling of information using various syntax notations and data serialization formats. The structure is formed by a set of *triplets* – each consting of a *subject*, a *predicate*, and an *object*. The set of *triplets* creates *RDF graph*.

RDF Schema. The *Resource Description Framework Schema* (RDF Schema or just RDFS) [8] is a semantic extension of RDF. It provides a data-modelling vocabulary for RDF data – a mechanism for describing groups of related resources and the relationships between these resources.

OWL. The W3C *Web Ontology Language* (OWL) [12] is a computational logic-based language. It is perceived as the first level above RDF required for the Semantic Web what can formally describe the meaning of the terminology used in Web documents. The knowledge expressed in OWL can be exploited by computer programs, e.g., to extend knowledge of the specific problem or to verify the consistency of specifically requested knowledge.

The basic building elements are *classes*, typically arranged in a *sub-class hierarchy*. Below, you can find an example (in *Turtle* notation) presented in [1]. Note, that OWL rely on *RDF Schema vocabulary* for the basic mechanism.

```
@prefix ex: <http://example.com/ns#> .
@prefix owl: <http://www.w3.org/2002/07/owl#> .
@prefix rdfs: <http://www.w3.org/2000/01/rdf−schema#> .

ex:Person
        a owl:Class ;
        rdfs:label "Person" ;
        rdfs:comment "A_human_being" .

ex:Customer
        a owl:Class ;
        rdfs:subClassOf ex:Person .
```

We introduced a sub-class *Customer* of parent class *Person*. In OWL notation, let us say that no *Person* can have more than one father.

```
@prefix ex: <http://example.com/ns#> .
@prefix owl: <http://www.w3.org/2002/07/owl#> .
@prefix rdfs: <http://www.w3.org/2000/01/rdf−schema#> .

ex:Person
        a owl:Class ;
        rdfs:subClassOf [
                a owl:Restriction ;
                owl:onProperty ex:hasFather ;
                owl:maxCardinality 1 ;
        ] ;
        rdfs:subClassOf [
                a owl:Restriction ;
                owl:onProperty ex:hasFather ;
                owl:allValuesFrom ex:Person ;
        ] .
```

OWL is operating on classes, which are understood as sets of instances that satisfy the same restrictions. OWL includes the metaclass `owl:Restriction` which is typically used as an anonymous superclass of the named class that the restriction is about [1].

SHACL. The *Shapes Constraint Language* (SHACL) is the new recommendation by W3C introduced in July 2017. The purpose of SHACL is to uniform both describing and constraining the content of the *RDF graph*. The set of constraints used by SHACL for validation are expressed as an RDF graph and are called *shapes* or *shape graphs* and the RDF data being validated is called the *data graph*. *Shapes* offer a description of the *data graph* in the form of *constraints* that a valid *data graph* satisfies [14].

Let us continue with the example above. SHACL offers in the way of restriction definition more flexibility. The equivalent of the previous example in SHACL language follows.

```
@prefix ex: <http://example.com/ns#> .
@prefix sh: <http://www.w3.org/ns/shacl#> .
@prefix owl: <http://www.w3.org/2002/07/owl#> .

ex:Person
        a owl:Class, sh:NodeShape ;
        sh:property [
                sh:path ex:hasFather ;
                sh:maxCount 1 ;
                sh:class ex:Person ;
        ] .
```

Another example of defining SHACL *shapes* is presented in [14]. Nice comparison of built-in constraint types is presented in [1].

2.3 Related Work Concerning Entity Extraction

In the context of entity extraction from the text, the current research is oriented on RDF *triplets*, e.g., [11], [15], or [6]. One can find also techniques about transformation from RDF *triplets* to SHACL *shapes*, e.g., in [9]. Our work differs in that we generate SHACL *shapes* directly from mapped parts of the text (via patterns presented in the next section).

There are also publications focused on the "reverse approach" concerning text descriptions generation from existing RDF *triplets*, e.g., [20] or [7].

3 Our Approach

In this contribution, we focus on *(sub)classes* and *properties* generation in SHACL language based on textual document. We also try to generate restrictions of properties, but only with a limitation to cardinality.

We reuse our approach of the *patterns* [16]. In the start phase of our project, we empirically identify patterns by processing various text documents (primarily using a source document of our experiment presented in the next section). Based on that, we were able to construct a *decision tree* as a final structure used in our implementation.

3.1 Suitable Patterns

Our implementation is written in Python based on *Spacy* NLP framework. The method of *grammatical inspection* uses typical NLP steps like *tokenization, sentence segmentation, part-of-speech tagging, lemmatization*, and *dependencies recognition* provided by the framework. Within the following examples of patterns, we use Penn Treebank [19] *part of speech* and *dependency* tags. The notation 0..* within connection link means, like in the E-R schema, that a target word with this connection does not have to exist or there can exist one word of a specific type, or there can exist more words of a specific type at the same time. Often, the subjects or the objects are represented by a composition of several nouns. Therefore, we introduce a shortened notation **NN*** means that at least one noun is required and there should also be more nouns composited via *compound* relation.

Class Specialization Pattern. Based on the following pattern (Fig. 1), the sentence *"The user is either a student or a teacher."* contains a class (*user*) and two sub-classes of this class (*student, teacher*). The matched parts of the pattern against the example sentence is illustrated in Fig. 2. The bold and coloured parts indicates matched parts.

126   D. Šenkýř

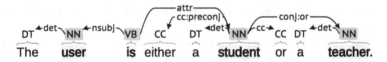

Fig. 1. The class specialization pattern

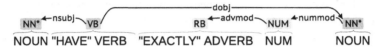

Fig. 2. The class specialization pattern matching example

Attributes Recognition Patterns. The patterns below focus determine the cardinality between class and their properties. The first attribute recognition pattern (Fig. 3) handles the adverb *exactly* that indicates the same minimal and maximal cardinality. The matching against example sentence *"Every user has exactly one username."* is illustrated in Fig. 4.

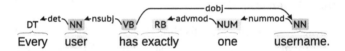

Fig. 3. The attribute recognition pattern #1

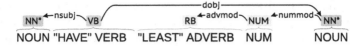

Fig. 4. The attribute recognition pattern #1 matching example

The second attribute recognition pattern (Fig. 5) handles the minimal cardinality in the form of word combination *at least*. The matching against example sentence *"Each student has at least one subject enrolled."* is illustrated in Fig. 6.

Fig. 5. The attribute recognition pattern #2

Fig. 6. The attribute recognition pattern #2 matching example

The third attribute recognition pattern (Fig. 7) combines the minimal and maximal cardinality. The matching against example sentence *"Each student has a minimum of 0 and a maximum of 150 credits."* is illustrated in Fig. 8.

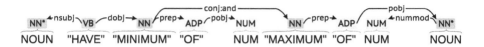

Fig. 7. The attribute recognition pattern #3

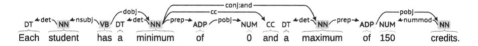

Fig. 8. The attribute recognition pattern #3 matching example

Experiment Result. The implemented algorithm keeps a collection of founded (sub)classes and their properties. This feature allows mapping of the resulting model sentence by sentence. With the usage of example sentences used in the patterns presentation above, in the end, the generated output in SHACL language should look like the following one.

```
@prefix ex: <http://example.com/ns#> .
@prefix sh: <http://www.w3.org/ns/shacl#> .
@prefix owl: <http://www.w3.org/2002/07/owl#> .
```

```
ex:User
   a owl:Class, sh:NodeShape ;
      sh:property [
         sh:path ex:hasUsername ;
         sh:minCount 1 ;
         sh:maxCount 1 ;
         sh:class ex:Username ;
   ] .
ex:Student
   a owl:Class, sh:NodeShape ;
      rdfs:subClassOf ex:User ;
      sh:property [
         sh:path ex:hasSubject ;
         sh:minCount 1 ;
         sh:class ex:Subject ;
      ] ;
      sh:property [
         sh:path ex:hasCredit ;
         sh:minCount 0 ;
         sh:maxCount 150 ;
         sh:class ex:Credit ;
      ] .
```

```
ex:Teacher
   a owl:Class .
   rdfs:subClassOf ex:User ;

ex:Username
   a owl:Class .

ex:Subject
   a owl:Class .

ex:Credit
   a owl:Class .
```

3.2 Ontology Resource Support

We argue that ordinary textual document suffers from the problem of incompleteness. That means that documents contain no proper or not complete description of entities, attributes, and relations. The author(s) forgot to mention it or the author(s) thought that some facts are best-known, and he or she did not explain them. The ontology database can support us here. We use *Schema.org*[5] API to get a collection of properties based on the entity (class) that we found in the text document. We remove properties that we extract from the text document and notify the user that there are some other properties that may forget to mention or that may be useful for him or her.

4 Conclusions

Using our sentence patterns defined above, we are able to generate the fragment of knowledge in SHACL language. With the help of ontology database, we can also inform the user that the generated fragment of SHACL *shape* may be extended. Our proposed method can be used in the very first phase of analysis of text documents.

In the context of theoretical implication, the direct generation (without the intermediate step of RDF generation and its transformation) offers the ability to tailor text sentence patterns to SHACL language strengths, e.g., the cardinality of properties. In the context of practical implication, the proposed method of NLP technique should be used as the back-end method of a text documents processing tool. The tool should process text sentence by sentence and at the same time also inform the user about a possible extension.

Acknowledgement. This research was supported by the grant of Czech Technical University in Prague No. SGS17/211/OHK3/3T/18.

References

1. SHACL and OWL Compared. http://spinrdf.org/shacl-and-owl.html. Accessed 08 Jan 2019
2. Arellano, A., Zontek-Carney, E., Austin, M.A.: Frameworks for natural language processing of textual requirements. Int. J. Adv. Syst. Meas. **8**, 230–240 (2015)
3. Auer, S., Bizer, C., Kobilarov, G., Lehmann, J., Cyganiak, R., Ives, Z.: DBpedia: a nucleus for a web of open data. In: Aberer, K., et al. (eds.) ASWC/ISWC -2007. LNCS, vol. 4825, pp. 722–735. Springer, Heidelberg (2007). https://doi.org/10.1007/978-3-540-76298-0_52
4. Ben Abdessalem Karaa, W., Ben Azzouz, Z., Singh, A., Dey, N., Ashour, A.S., Ben Ghazala, H.: Automatic builder of class diagram (ABCD): an application of UML generation from functional requirements. Softw. Pract. Exp. **46**(11), 1443–1458 (2016)

---

[5] https://schema.org.

5. Cyganiak, R., Wood, D., Lanthaler, M.: RDF 1.1 concepts and Abstract Syntax. W3C recommendation, W3C (2014). http://www.w3.org/TR/2014/REC-rdf11-concepts-20140225

6. Draicchio, F., Gangemi, A., Presutti, V., Nuzzolese, A.G.: FRED: from natural language text to RDF and OWL in one click. In: Cimiano, P., Fernández, M., Lopez, V., Schlobach, S., Völker, J. (eds.) ESWC 2013. LNCS, vol. 7955, pp. 263–267. Springer, Heidelberg (2013). https://doi.org/10.1007/978-3-642-41242-4_36

7. Gardent, C., Shimorina, A., Narayan, S., Perez-Beltrachini, L.: The WebNLG challenge: generating text from RDF data. In: Proceedings of the 10th International Conference on Natural Language Generation, Spain, pp. 124–133. Association for Computational Linguistics, Santiago de Compostela (2017)

8. Guha, R., Brickley, D.: RDF Schema 1.1. W3C recommendation, W3C (2014). http://www.w3.org/TR/2014/REC-rdf-schema-20140225/

9. Irene, P.: From OWL to SHACL in an automated way. https://www.topquadrant.com/2018/05/01/from-owl-to-shacl-in-an-automated-way (2018). Accessed 19 May 2019

10. Landhäußer, M., Körner, S.J., Tichy, W.F.: From requirements to UML models and back: how automatic processing of text can support requirements engineering. Softw. Qual. J. **22**(1), 121–149 (2014)

11. Martinez-Rodriguez, J.L., Lopez-Arevalo, I., Rios-Alvarado, A.B., Hernandez, J., Aldana-Bobadilla, E.: Extraction of RDF statements from text. In: Villazón-Terrazas, B., Hidalgo-Delgado, Y. (eds.) KGSWC 2019. CCIS, vol. 1029, pp. 87–101. Springer, Cham (2019). https://doi.org/10.1007/978-3-030-21395-4_7

12. McGuinness, D., van Harmelen, F.: OWL Web Ontology Language Overview. W3C recommendation, W3C (2004). http://www.w3.org/TR/2004/REC-owl-features-20040210

13. Mylopoulos, J.: Conceptual Modelling and Telos. Conceptual Modelling, Databases and CASE: An Integrated View of Information System Development. Wiley, New York (1992)

14. Pandit, H.J., O'Sullivan, D., Lewis, D.: Using ontology design patterns to define SHACL shapes. In: Proceedings of the 9th Workshop on Ontology Design and Patterns (WOP 2018) Co-located with 17th International Semantic Web Conference (ISWC 2018), pp. 67–71 (2018)

15. Perera, R., Nand, P., Klette, G.: RealText-lex: a lexicalization framework for RDF triples. Prague Bull. Math. Linguist. **106**(1), 45–68 (2016)

16. Šenkýř, D., Kroha, P.: Patterns in textual requirements specification. In: Proceedings of the 13th International Conference on Software Technologies, Porto, Portugal, pp. 197–204. SCITEPRESS - Science and Technology Publications (2018)

17. Speer, R., Havasi, C.: Representing General Relational Knowledge in ConceptNet 5. In: Proceedings of the Eighth International Conference on Language Resources and Evaluation (LREC-2012). European Language Resources Association (ELRA) (2012)

18. Staab, S., Lehmann, J., Verborgh, R.: Structured knowledge on the Web 7.0. In: Companion of the The Web Conference 2018 on The Web Conference 2018 - WWW 2018, Lyon, France, pp. 885–886. ACM Press (2018)

19. Taylor, A., Marcus, M., Santorini, B.: The Penn Treebank: an overview. In: Abeillé, A. (ed.) Treebanks. Text, Speech and Language Technolog, vol. 20, pp. 5–22. Springer, Dordrecht (2003). https://doi.org/10.1007/978-94-010-0201-1_1

20. Trisedya, B.D., Qi, J., Zhang, R., Wang, W.: GTR-LSTM: a triple encoder for sentence generation from RDF data. In: Proceedings of the 56th Annual Meeting of the Association for Computational Linguistics, Melbourne, Australia, vol. 1, pp. 1627–1637. Association for Computational Linguistics (2018)
21. Verdonck, M., Gailly, F., Pergl, R., Guizzardi, G., Martins, B., Pastor, O.: Comparing traditional conceptual modeling with ontology-driven conceptual modeling: an empirical study. Inf. Syst. **81**, 92–103 (2019)

Detection of Declarative Process Constraints in LTL Formulas

Nicolai Schützenmeier$^{(\boxtimes)}$, Martin Käppel, Sebastian Petter, Stefan Schönig, and Stefan Jablonski

Institute for Computer Science, University of Bayreuth, Bayreuth, Germany
{nicolai.schuetzenmeier,martin.kaeppel,sebastian.petter, stefan.schoenig,stefan.jablonski}@uni-bayreuth.de

Abstract. Declarative process models consist of temporal constraints that a process must satisfy during execution. Constraint templates are patterns that define parameterized classes of properties. Their semantics can be formalized using formal logics such as Linear Temporal Logic (LTL) over finite traces. There exists a big amount of different constraint templates for different purposes. In practice, the variety of different templates yields complexity and performance issues with regard to model comparison, compliance checking and in particular process mining. In this paper we give a comprehensively overview about existing declare templates and transform their underlying LTL formula into the positive normal form (PNF), a canonical standard form for LTL formulas. On this basis, we present an algorithm for detecting declare templates in any LTL formula fulfilling the conditions for PNF. We reduce the number of process constraints that have to be proven by the algorithm to speed up the runtime and give some advice for further optimizations.

Keywords: Declarative process management · Declare · Linear temporal logic · Positive normal form

1 Introduction

A Process-Aware Information System is a collaborative system that executes processes involving people, applications, and data on the basis of process models [1]. Two different paradigms can be distinguished: *(i)* procedural models describe the execution paths in a graph-based structure, *(ii)* declarative models consist of temporal constraints that a process must satisfy. Declarative languages like Declare [2], DCR graphs [3], and Declarative Process Intermediate Language (DPIL) [4,5] have been proposed to define the latter.

Declarative models represent processes by restrictions over the permissible behaviour. The restricting rules are named constraints, which express those conditions that must be satisfied throughout process execution. Modeling languages like Declare [2] provide a repertoire of templates, i.e., constraints parametrized over activities. Therefore Declare templates are represented by a formula in

© Springer Nature Switzerland AG 2019
R. Pergl et al. (Eds.): EOMAS 2019, LNBIP 366, pp. 131–145, 2019.
https://doi.org/10.1007/978-3-030-35646-0_10

Linear Temporal Logic (LTL) [6]. As an LTL formula is not unique, in literature there are often different representations of the same Declare template [7,8]. Hence, it is more difficult to compare two process models and to work out common properties. In this paper we transform each formula into the Positive Normal Form (PNF) [9], a unique standard form for LTL formulas.

Based on the PNF, we develop and implement an algorithm to detect Declare templates in any LTL formula fulfilling the conditions for PNF. Therefore, we build a binary tree and search through this tree to discover the known Declare templates using the fact that templates occur as subtrees.

This algorithm can be used to compare process models. As an introductory example we consider the *choice* template. *choice*(A, B) means that in the process execution at least activity A or activity B has to be executed. In other words: activity A or activity B has to occur. This yields to the fact that the *choice* template can be expressed by two *existence* templates using a disjunctive connective:

$$choice(A, B) = existence(A) \lor existence(B).$$

In general, a model checker would not find the common property of two different process models using the described representations of the same fact. Our approach is to handle this problem and to give an algorithm to detect these *hidden* properties of process models.

The remainder of the paper is structured as follows: Sect. 2 gives an overview about related work. In Sect. 3 we introduce Declare and the most common used templates. In Sect. 4 we present the PNF and transform the LTL formulas behind the Declare templates into the PNF. In Sect. 5 we introduce our approach and the implementation of the algorithm. In Sect. 6 we give some ideas for further optimizations. In the last Section we conclude the main results of this paper.

2   Related Work

Linear Temporal Logic (LTL) [10] specifications are traditionally used for expressing the properties that a reactive system should exhibit or avoid. The specifications are exploited by model checking tools for formal verification (e.g., [11]). However, LTL has also been used to conceptually define process models in Business Process Management (BPM). Declarative process modeling languages like Declare [12], i.e. the ConDec language [8] adopt LTL to model business processes, business rules and policies. The resulting LTL formula is then converted to an automaton for execution [2]. In [13] semantics for defining Declare constraints on non-atomic activities and an approach for the discovery of this type of constraints are presented. Declare only constrains the starts of activities and interrelates them temporally. Data oriented aspects and the organizational perspective [14] are completely missing in traditional Declare. The approaches proposed in [15,16] allow for the specification of constraints that go beyond the traditional Declare templates. In [17], the authors define *Timed Declare*, an extension of Declare that relies on timed automata. In [18], the authors introduce for the first time a data aware semantics for Declare. In [19]

Table 1. Semantics for Declare constraints in LTL_f.

Template	LTL_f Semantics
existence(A)	$\mathbf{F}(A)$
absence(A)	$\neg\mathbf{F}(A)$
atLeast(A, n)	$\mathbf{F}(A \wedge \mathbf{X}(\text{atLeast}(A, n-1)))$, atLeast($A, 1$) $= \mathbf{F}(A)$
atMost(A, n)	$\mathbf{G}(\neg A \vee \mathbf{X}(\text{atMost}(A, n-1)))$, atMost($A, 0$) $= \mathbf{G}(\neg A)$
init(A)	A
last(A)	$\mathbf{G}(\neg A \rightarrow \mathbf{F}(A))$
respondedExistence(A, B)	$\mathbf{F}(A) \rightarrow \mathbf{F}(B)$
response(A, B)	$\mathbf{G}(A \rightarrow \mathbf{F}(B))$
alternateResponse(A, B)	$\mathbf{G}(A \rightarrow \mathbf{X}(\neg A\mathbf{U}B))$
chainResponse(A, B)	$\mathbf{G}(A \rightarrow \mathbf{X}(B))$
precedence(A, B)	$\mathbf{F}(B) \rightarrow ((\neg B)\mathbf{U}A)$
alternatePrecedence(A, B)	precedence(A, B) $\wedge \mathbf{G}(B \rightarrow \mathbf{X}(\text{precedence}(A, B)))$
chainPrecedence(A, B)	precedence(A, B) $\wedge \mathbf{G}(\mathbf{X}(B) \rightarrow A)$
succession(A, B)	response(A, B) $\wedge$ precedence(A, B)
chainSuccession(A, B)	$\mathbf{G}(A \leftrightarrow \mathbf{X}(B))$
alternateSuccession(A, B)	alternateResponse(A, B) $\wedge$ alternatePrecedence(A, B)
notSuccession(A, B)	$\mathbf{G}(A \rightarrow \neg\mathbf{F}(B))$
notChainSuccession(A, B)	$\mathbf{G}(A \rightarrow \neg\mathbf{X}(B))$
notRespondedExistence(A, B)	$\mathbf{F}(A) \rightarrow \mathbf{F}(B)$
notResponse(A, B)	$\mathbf{G}(A \rightarrow \neg\mathbf{F}(B))$
notPrecedence(A, B)	$\mathbf{G}(F(B) \rightarrow \neg A)$
notChainResponse	$\mathbf{G}(A \rightarrow \neg\mathbf{X}(B))$
notChainPrecedence(A, B)	$\mathbf{G}(\mathbf{X}(B) \rightarrow \neg A)$
coExistence(A, B)	$\mathbf{F}(A) \leftrightarrow \mathbf{F}(B)$
notCoExistence(A, B)	$\neg(\mathbf{F}(A) \wedge \mathbf{F}(B))$
choice(A, B)	$\mathbf{F}(A) \vee \mathbf{F}(B)$
exclusiveChoice(A, B)	$(\mathbf{F}(A) \vee \mathbf{F}(B)) \wedge \neg(\mathbf{F}(A) \wedge \mathbf{F}(B))$

a general multi perspective LTL semantics for Declare (*MP-Declare*) has been presented. Here, Declare is extented with elements of first order logic to refer to data values in constraints. Data aware as well as generalized MP-Declare models are supported in the context of conformance checking [19], process discovery [20] and trace generation [21,22]. Recently, the authors presented an approach for executing MP-Declare specifications [23]. To best of our knowledge the PNF was not applied in context of Declare Process Constraints until now.

3   Declare

Declarative constraints are well-suited for representing the permissible behaviour of business processes. Modeling languages like Declare [24] describe a set of *constraints* that must be satisfied throughout the process execution. Constraints, in turn, are instances of predefined *templates*. Templates, in turn, are patterns that define parameterized classes of properties. Their semantics can be formalized using formal logics such as Linear Temporal Logic over finite traces (LTL_f) [25].

The $\mathbf{F}$, $\mathbf{X}$, $\mathbf{G}$, $\mathbf{W}$ and $\mathbf{U}$ LTL_f future operators have the following meanings: formula $\mathbf{F}\psi_1$ means that ψ_1 holds sometime in the future, $\mathbf{X}\psi_1$ means that ψ_1 holds in the next position, $\mathbf{G}\psi_1$ says that ψ_1 holds forever in the future, and, lastly, $\psi_1\mathbf{U}\psi_2$ means that sometime in the future ψ_2 will hold and until that moment ψ_1 holds (with ψ_1 and ψ_2 LTL_f formulas). There is a weaker form of the until operator, so called *weak until* $\psi_1\mathbf{W}\psi_2$, where the second formula ψ_2 is not required to hold. In this case, the first formula ψ_1 must hold forever.

In general, we distinguish between two types of templates: *unary* and *binary* templates. Unary templates refer to one activity, e.g. the *existence* template $\mathbf{F}(A)$ means that activity A has to occur in the process execution. So this template only refers to activity A. On the other side, we consider the *response* constraint $\mathbf{G}(A \rightarrow \mathbf{F}(B))$. It indicates that if A *occurs*, B must eventually *follow*. So it refers to the activities A and B. Therefore, this constraint is fully satisfied in traces such as $t_1 = \langle A, A, B, C\rangle$, $t_2 = \langle B, B, C, D\rangle$, and $t_3 = \langle A, B, C, B\rangle$, but not for $t_4 = \langle A, B, A, C\rangle$ because the second occurrence of A is not followed by a B. In t_2, it is *vacuously satisfied* [26], in a trivial way, because A never occurs. Table 1 gives an overview about the most important Declare templates.

4   Transformation of Declare Templates

Any LTL formula can be transformed into a canonical form, the Positive Normal Form (PNF). These formulas are a syntactically restricted subset of LTL formulas in which the use of negation ($\neg$) is allowed only immediately in front of atomic propositions [27,28]. The PNF is strongly related to disjunctive and conjunctive normalform that are special cases of PNF. For the transformation of an LTL formula into PNF, for each LTL-operator a dual operator is needed [27].

Hence, for the constant **true** we need to consider the constant **false**, for the conjunction connective ($\wedge$) we need to consider the disjunctive connective ($\vee$). The operator $\mathbf{X}$ is dual to itself. Finally we have to consider the $\mathbf{U}$ operator. We observe that

$$\neg\,(\phi\,\mathbf{U}\,\psi) \equiv ((\phi \wedge \neg\psi)\,\mathbf{U}\,(\neg\phi \wedge \neg\psi)) \vee \mathbf{G}\,(\phi \wedge \neg\psi) \equiv (\phi \wedge \neg\psi)\,\mathbf{W}\,(\neg\phi \wedge \neg\psi)$$
$$\neg\,(\phi\,\mathbf{W}\,\psi) \equiv (\phi \wedge \neg\psi)\,\mathbf{U}\,(\neg\phi \wedge \neg\psi)\,.$$

Thus there is a duality between $\mathbf{W}$ and $\mathbf{U}$. Consider that $\mathbf{G}$ and $\mathbf{F}$ can be expressed by

$$\mathbf{G}\phi \equiv \phi\,\mathbf{W}\,\textbf{false}$$
$$\mathbf{F}\phi \equiv \textbf{true}\,\mathbf{U}\,\phi.$$

Table 2. Declare constraints Positive Normal Form.

Template	Positive Normal Form
existence(A)	true $\mathbf{U}\,A$
absence(A)	false $\mathbf{U}\neg A$
atLeast(A, n)	true $\mathbf{U}(A \wedge \mathbf{X}(\text{atLeast}(A, n - 1))$
atMost(A, n)	$(\neg A \vee \mathbf{X}(\text{atMost}(A, n - 1)))\mathbf{W}$false
init(A)	A
last(A)	$(A \vee (\text{true}\mathbf{U}A))\mathbf{W}$false
respondedExistence(A, B)	$(\neg A\mathbf{W}\text{false}) \vee (\text{true}\mathbf{U}B)$
response(A, B)	$(\neg A \vee (\text{true}\mathbf{U}B))\mathbf{W}$false
alternateResponse(A, B)	$(\neg A \vee \mathbf{X}(\neg A\mathbf{U}B))\mathbf{W}$false
chainResponse(A, B)	$(\neg A \vee \mathbf{X}(B))\mathbf{W}$false
precedence(A, B)	$\neg B\mathbf{W}A$
alternatePrecedence(A, B)	$(\neg B\mathbf{W}A) \wedge ((\neg B \vee \mathbf{X}(\neg B\mathbf{W}A)))\mathbf{W}$false
chainPrecedence(A, B)	$(\neg B\mathbf{W}A) \wedge ((\mathbf{X}(\neg B) \vee A)\mathbf{W}$false$)$
succession(A, B)	$(\neg A \vee (\text{true}\mathbf{U}B))\mathbf{W}$false $\wedge \neg B\mathbf{W}A$
chainSuccession(A, B)	$((A \wedge \mathbf{X}(B)) \vee (\neg A \wedge \mathbf{X}(\neg B)))\mathbf{W}$false
alternateSuccession(A, B)	$(\neg A \vee \mathbf{X}(\neg A\mathbf{U}B))\mathbf{W}$false $\wedge (\neg B\mathbf{W}A) \wedge ((\neg B \vee \mathbf{X}(\neg B\mathbf{W}A)))\mathbf{W}$false
notSuccession(A, B)	$(\neg A \vee (\neg B\mathbf{W}\text{false}))\mathbf{W}$false
notChainSuccession(A, B)	$(\neg A \vee \mathbf{X}(\neg B))\mathbf{W}$false
notRespondedExistence(A, B)	$(\neg A\mathbf{W}\text{false}) \vee (\neg B\mathbf{W}\text{false})$
notResponse(A, B)	$(\neg A \vee (\neg B\mathbf{W}\text{false}))\mathbf{W}$false
notPrecedence(A, B)	$((\neg B\mathbf{W}\text{false}) \vee \neg A)\mathbf{W}$false
notChainResponse	$(\neg A \vee \mathbf{X}(\neg B))\mathbf{W}$false
notChainPrecedence(A, B)	$(\mathbf{X}(\neg B) \vee \neg A)\mathbf{W}$false
coExistence(A, B)	$((\text{true}\mathbf{U}A) \wedge (\text{true}\mathbf{U}B)) \vee ((\neg A\mathbf{W}\text{false}) \wedge (\neg B\mathbf{W}\text{false}))$
notCoExistence(A, B)	$(\neg A\mathbf{W}\text{false}) \vee (\neg B\mathbf{W}\text{false})$
choice(A, B)	$(\text{true}\mathbf{U}A) \vee (\text{true}\mathbf{U}B)$
exclusiveChoice(A, B)	$((\text{true}\mathbf{U}A) \vee (\text{true}\mathbf{U}B)) \wedge ((\neg A\mathbf{W}\text{false}) \vee (\neg B\mathbf{W}\text{false}))$

Consequently the set of LTL-operators for PNF is restricted to $\mathbf{X}$, $\mathbf{U}$, and $\mathbf{W}$. Finally we can define the set of LTL formulas in PNF by [29]

$$\phi ::= \mathbf{true} \mid \mathbf{false} \mid a \mid \neg a \mid \phi_1 \wedge \phi_2 \mid \phi_1 \vee \phi_2 \mid \mathbf{X}\,\phi \mid \phi_1\,\mathbf{U}\,\phi_2 \mid \phi_1\,\mathbf{W}\,\phi_2.$$

We can transform an LTL formula into PNF by using the common LTL transformations. As an example we transform the *notChainPrecedence(A,B)* template into PNF:

$$\mathbf{G}\,(\mathbf{X}\,(B) \to \neg A) \equiv (\mathbf{X}\,(B) \to \neg A)\,\mathbf{W}\,\mathbf{false} \equiv (\neg\mathbf{X}(B) \vee \neg A)\,\mathbf{W}\,\mathbf{false}$$
$$\equiv (\mathbf{X}\,(\neg B) \vee \neg A)\,\mathbf{W}\,\mathbf{false}.$$

Analogously we transform all Declare templates from Table 1 into PNF as shown in Table 2. For correct understanding we recall to the operator hierarchy for LTL formulas: A unary operator binds stronger than a binary operator and $\mathbf{U}$ takes precedence over $\wedge$, $\vee$, and $\to$. For the ease of use and better readability we enrich the formulas by extensive use of brackets.

In literature the LTL representation of Declare templates differs. Often past operators ($\mathbf{O}$, $\mathbf{Y}$, $\mathbf{S}$), which are not part of LTL are used for ease of use. In PNF the set of operators is reduced and all formulas are built in the same way. In combination with the uniqueness of PNF this leads to a strong simplification of formula comparison and template detection. Furthermore there is a large number of approaches for the theoretical analysis of logic formulas based on PNF (e. g. classification of languages and their expressiveness). However, the transformation of a formula into PNF can lead to an exponential grow in length due to the translation of the until operator [28].

5   Approach and Implementation

Our goal is to transform any LTL formula in PNF into a composition of known Declare templates. Therefore we first transform all known Declare templates into binary trees in XML format to simplify the recognition of these templates. Our approach is to get a valid PNF formula as string as user-input, transform this string into a binary tree and subsequently replace all subtrees which are equal to one of the template trees.

At first we define a grammar for the Xtext framework[1] to parse the input string to a binary tree. The grammar is based on the PNF with one additional restriction: the position of the brackets. Every formula is a three tuple and contains a left element, an operator and a right element. A general formula is structured as follows:

$$(left : [\text{Activity}|\text{Formula}] \; op : \text{Operator} \; right : [\text{Activity}| \; \text{Formula}]). \quad (1)$$

The operator is one of the four input operators, namely $\wedge, \vee, \mathbf{W}$ or $\mathbf{U}$. The left and the right element can be either another formula or an activity. Every formula is surrounded by an opening and a closing bracket with an optional LTL $\mathbf{X}$-operator preceded. An activity can be any string with an optional $\neg$ beforehand. In addition, it is possible to write $\mathbf{X}$(activity) instead of the activity only.

After defining the grammar we write a code generator in Xtend to transform the valid input string into an unique XML binary tree so we can subsequently check for template appearances. The tree is built up from a formula as binary tree where the operator of the formula is represented as node and the left and the right element are the left respectively the right leaf.

With help of this code generator we are able to create a binary tree from every input formula. We create an XML binary tree from each template in Table 2 by using the discovered PNF formulas. As an example we show the result of the response template used as input. Figure 1 shows the resulting tree in XML representation and visualizes the tree. To simplify the subtree algorithm every node gets a unique ID as well as a customized value. Every activity is surrounded by two # symbols. The $\neg$ operator is replaced by _not_ and true/false are written as _true_ respectively _false_.

---

[1] https://www.eclipse.org/Xtext/.

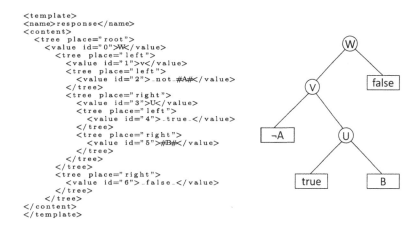

```
<template>
  <name>response</name>
  <content>
    <tree place="root">
      <value id="0">W</value>
        <tree place="left">
          <value id="1">v</value>
            <tree place="left">
              <value id="2">_not_#A#</value>
            </tree>
            <tree place="right">
              <value id="3">U</value>
                <tree place="left">
                  <value id="4">_true_</value>
                </tree>
                <tree place="right">
                  <value id="5">#B#</value>
                </tree>
            </tree>
        </tree>
        <tree place="right">
          <value id="6">_false_</value>
        </tree>
    </tree>
  </content>
</template>
```

Fig. 1. XML representation and corresponding binary tree for the *response* template

The greatest challenge for template detection is the handling of commutative and distributive laws for the conjunction and disjunctive connectives. The *last(A)* template, for example, can be written in PNF either as

$$(A \vee (\textbf{true U } A)) \textbf{ W false} \text{ or}$$
$$((\textbf{true U } A) \vee A) \textbf{ W false}.$$

In some cases the underlying PNF formula contains a formula similar to $A \vee (B \wedge C)$. Hence, $(A \vee B) \wedge (A \vee C)$ would be an equivalent form due to the distributive law. Obviously there is additionally the possibility to apply the distributive law together with the commutative law. With regard to flexibility and expandability the algorithm should be able to detect all these representations without a hard encoding of all variants. Obviously the detection of templates becomes more difficult. In the following implementation, we will only focus on the handling of the commutative law and leave the distributive law to the Xtext framework.

Analogously to the input formula ϕ_i we build a binary tree for every Declare template. We define the *length* l_ϕ of a PNF formula ϕ as the number of nodes in the corresponding binary tree. It means the length of a formula denotes the number of atomic propositions, operators, connectives, and constants (true and false) in the formula. Consider, for example, the *response* template has a length of 7 (two atomic proposition, two constants, two operators and one disjunctive connective). We compare the length l_t of a Declare template t to the length l_{ϕ_i} of the input formula to avoid unnecessary checks. Note that this method works independently of the number of brackets or the name of their atomic propositions. During the transformation into a binary tree, we store the IDs of the nodes that represent a conjunction or disjunctive connective. We denote this set of IDs as O_t. Under abuse of notation we use in the pseudocode the same notation for formula and binary tree. Nevertheless this notation is acceptable because of the possibility to transform a formula into a binary tree and vice versa.

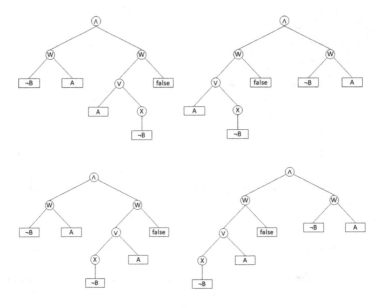

Fig. 2. Four swap trees of the *chainPrecedence* template

For the detection of a template we generate all possible variants of its under-lying PNF formula with regard to the names of the atomic propositions in the input formula. A *variant* of a template means the resulting binary tree after the application of commutative or distributive laws or the renaming of the atomic propositions. We generate the variants in two consecutive steps. In the first step, the so called *denomination step*, we rename the atomic propositions according to the names of the atomic propositions in the input formula (see Algorithm 3). Afterwards we apply commutative laws on the resulting trees from the previous step (so called *swapping step*). The swapping step is presented in Algorithm 4 and illustrated in Fig. 2.

As preparation of the denomination step we extract the names of the atomic propositions in the input formula using the fact that they are surrounded by #. We denote this set as A_{ϕ_i}. We have to distinguish between unary and binary Declare templates. If the template is unary, we prove its occurrence for all atomic proposition of ϕ_i. If the template is binary, every $a \in A_{\phi_i}$ must act once as first parameter and once as second parameter of the template. Hence, we need all two elementary subsets of A_{ϕ_i} with respect to the ordering. We illustrate the denomination step with a simple example. Assume that the input formula ϕ_i contains three atomic propositions and that we want to prove whether ϕ_i contains the unary *existence* and the binary *response* template. It means $A_{\phi_i} = \{A, B, C\}$. First we prove the containment of *existence(A)*, *existence(B)*, and *existence(C)*. For the *response* template we have to consider the following sets: $(A, B), (B, A), (A, C), (C, A), (B, C)$, and (C, B).

In the swapping step we generate new variants by applying the commu-tative law on all variants from the denomination step. The number of such

---

Algorithm 1. Check the occurence of all templates

Data: set of templates $\tilde{T}$, Input formula ϕ_i
1 **for** $t \in \tilde{T}$ **do**
    /* call Algorithm 2   */
2   checkTemplate(t, ϕ_i)
3 **end**

Algorithm 2. Check the occurence of a specific template

Data: Template t, Input formula ϕ_i
    /* Extract commutative positions from t */
1 $O_t \leftarrow$ extractCommutativePositions(t)
2 variations $\leftarrow \emptyset$
    /* Extract atomic propositions from ϕ_i */
3 $A_{\phi_i} \leftarrow$ extractPropositions(ϕ_i)
4 **if** $t.length \leq \phi_i.length$ **then**
    /* Denomination step, call Algorithm 3   */
5   variations $\leftarrow$ denominationStep(t, A_{ϕ_i})
6   allVariations $\leftarrow \emptyset$
    /* Swapping step, call Algorithm 4   */
7   **for** $v \in$ *variations* **do**
        /* Looping over the power set of commutativePositions$_t$ */
8   **for** $p \in \mathcal{P}(O_t)$ **do**
9   allVariations.add(swap(v,p))
10   **end**
11   **end**
12   **for** $v \in$ *allVariations* **do**
13   isSubtree(ϕ_i,v)
14   **end**
15 **end**

---

transformations is equal to the cardinality of the power set of O_t minus one. The minus one is necessary because the empty set describes no transformation. We can use O_t for all variants because renaming the atomic propositions in the previous step does not effect the node's ID. By means of the notation of binary trees, applying the commutative law, means swapping left and right child of a node that contains a conjunctive or disjunctive connective.

After this type of preprocessing we start with the template detection. We use the fact that if a formula in PNF contains a Declare template, it occurs as a subtree. So the problem is reduced to the well known subtree problem. Hence it is sufficient to run a subtree algorithm on the corresponding binary tree of the input formula for all variants of the template. The subtree algorithm (see Algorithm 5) should not only answer the question whether the template occurs, however it should give the positions and the number of occurrences.

Algorithm 3. Denomination step

Data: Template t, set of atomic propositions A_{ϕ_i}
Result: Set of variations

```
 1  variations ← ∅
 2  for a ∈ A_φi do
       /* Replace all node names #A# in the binary tree t with a    */
 3   |   variations.add(replace(#A#, a, t))
 4  end
 5  subset ← twoElementarySubsetsOf(A_φi)
 6  for k ∈ subset do
 7   |   tempTree ← replace(#A#, k.firstElement, t)
 8   |   variations.add(replace(#B#, k.secondElement, tempTree))
 9   |   tempTree ← replace(#B#, k.firstElement, t)
10   |   variations.add(replace(#A#, k.secondElement, tempTree))
11  end
12  return variations
```

Our subtree algorithm is based on pre- and inorder traversal of the involved binary trees. We denote the preorder traversal of a binary tree T as *preOrder(T)* and analogously the inorder traversal as *inOrder(T)*. A binary tree S is a subtree of T if the *preOrder(S)* is a substring of *preOrder(T)* and *inorder(S)* is a substring of *inOrder(T)*.

We use an own modification of the Knuth-Morris-Pratt-Algorithm [30] for string matching that works on whole words instead of single characters. The nodes of preorder and inorder traversal of both trees are stored in arrays. Afterwards the matching algorithm is applied to these arrays by comparing the names of the nodes. Working on arrays is beneficial because the starting position of the matching corresponds directly to a node. Hence, we can easily extract the ID in inorder traversal which describes the root node of the subtree.

Based on that fact we can give an extension for simplifying the input formula. At first we search for every match the root node of the subtree. Afterwards we rename these nodes with the name of the found templates and remove the left and right childs. After running the algorithm on all templates, the binary tree is a simplified version of the input formula. It is not difficult to transform this binary tree back into the formula representation.

A full runtime analysis of our algorithm is difficult because of the large number of auxiliary algorithms like the power set or the string matching algorithm. Furthermore there are several implementations or other algorithms that work as well as our proposed algorithms. Hence, we only determine the number of variations that have to be checked. We denote the set of templates as $T = \{t_1, ..., t_d\}$, the number of atomic propositions in the input formula ϕ_i as n, and the number of commutative positions of a template t_i as c_{t_i}. For the determination of the number of variations it is sufficient to analyze the denomination and swapping

---

Algorithm 4. Generates variants based on commutative law for conjunctive and disjunctive connectives

---

Data: Variation v, Set of positions p
Result: Swapped tree according to positions p

```
1  swappedTree ← v
2  if p.isEmpty then
3  |    return swappedTree
4  else
5  |    for i ∈ p do
          /* Search node in swappedTree with ID p.id          */
6  |    |    result ← searchNodeWithID(swappedTree, p.id)
          /* Change left and right child of the result node   */
7  |    |    temp ← result.rightChild
8  |    |    result.rightChild ← result.leftChild
9  |    |    result.leftChild ← temp
10 |    end
11 |    return swappedTree
12 end
```

---

step in depth. The number of variations v can be calculated by:

$$v = \sum_{i=1}^{d} \left(n + \binom{n}{2} \cdot 2 \right) \cdot 2^{c_{t_i}} = \sum_{i=1}^{d} \left(n + \frac{n!}{2 \cdot (n-2)!} \cdot 2 \right) \cdot 2^{c_{t_i}}$$

$$= \sum_{i=1}^{d} (n + n(n-1)) \cdot 2^{c_{t_i}} = n^2 \cdot \sum_{i=1}^{d} 2^{c_{t_i}}.$$

This formula describes the worst case, where the length of ϕ_i is greater than or equal to the length of each template. This is realistic for large Declare Process Models.

6 Optimization and Further Work

In this section we want to give some advice for possible optimizations. Therefore we decrease the number of templates that are checked on existence in the tree in Sect. 5.

At first we can leave off the *choice* template because this one just consists of two *existence* templates and a disjunctive connective:

$$choice(A, B) = existence(A) \vee existence(B)$$

Due to this fact we do not have to look for the *choice* template in the LTL formulas.

A second improvement is to replace the *atLeast* template by a specification of the *atMost* template. We claim:

$$atLeast(A, n) = \neg atMost(A, n-1) \tag{2}$$

Algorithm 5. Subtree algorithm

  Data: Binary tree T, Binary Tree S
  Result: Whether S is a subtree of T
1 **if** $S.length = 0$ **then**
2 | **return** true
3 **end**
4 **if** $T.length = 0$ **then**
5 | **return** false
6 **end**
7 **if** $T.Length \geq S.length$ **then**
  | /* Arrays with the names for node traversal   */
8 | tInOrder[ ] ← inOrder(T)
9 | sInOrder[ ] ← inOrder(S)
10 | tPreOrder[ ] ← preOrder(T)
11 | sPreOrder[ ] ← preOrder(S)
  | /* String matching on arrays, returns positions and prints wheter T
  | containts variation S */
12 | listOccurencesPre = KnuthMorrisPrattAlgorithm(tPreOrder, sPreOrder)
13 | listOccurencesIn = KnuthMorrisPrattAlgorithm(tInOrder, sInOrder)
14 | **if** listOccurencesPre.$size > 0$ and listOccurencesIn.$size > 0$ **then**
  | | /* There you can insert a by optional simplification step for T
  | | by iterating over listOccurencesIn   */
15 | | **return** true
16 | **else**
17 | | **return** false
18 | **end**
19 **else**
20 | **return** false
21 **end**

We prove the claim (1) in the following by induction over n.
We first show that (1) holds for the base case $n = 1$:

$$atLeast(A, 1) = \mathbf{F}(A) = \neg\neg\mathbf{F}(A) = \neg\mathbf{G}(\neg A) = \neg atMost(A, 0)$$

So formula (1) holds for $n = 1$.

Our induction hypothesis is that (1) holds for any $n \in \mathbb{N}$. We have to show that

$$atLeast(A, n + 1) = \neg atMost(A, n).$$

By using the induction hypothesis (1) we get:

$$atLeast(A, n + 1) = \mathbf{F}(A \wedge \mathbf{X}(atLeast(A, n))) = \mathbf{F}(A \wedge \mathbf{X}(\neg atMost(A, n - 1)))$$

Further transformations lead finally to:

$$\mathbf{F}(A \wedge \mathbf{X}(\neg atMost(A, n - 1))) = \neg\mathbf{G}(\neg A \vee \neg\mathbf{X}(\neg atMost(A, n - 1))) =$$
$$= \neg\mathbf{G}(\neg A \vee \mathbf{X}(atMost(A, n - 1))) = \neg atMost(A, n)$$

$\square$

Further optimization would be to find similar equations or properties. Every single correlation between constraints decreases the runtime of the in Sect. 5 introduced algorithm.

7   Conclusion

In this paper we transform Declare templates into the PNF. Using the fact that the PNF is unique for LTL formulas, we present an algorithm to detect Declare templates in any LTL formula fulfilling the conditions for the PNF. Therefore we use several different techniques, e.g. subtree algorithms or pattern matching. With the introduced algorithm it is much easier to compare different process models and to work out common properties. We finally give some advice for further optimizations to decrease the runtime of the developed algorithm.

References

1. Dumas, M., Rosa, M.L., Mendling, J., Reijers, H.A.: Fundamentals of Business Process Management, 2nd edn. Springer, Heidelberg (2018). https://doi.org/10.1007/978-3-662-56509-4
2. Pesic, M., Schonenberg, H., van der Aalst, W.M.P.: Declare: full support for loosely-structured processes. In: IEEE EDOC Conference 2007, pp. 287–300 (2007)
3. Hildebrandt, T.T., Mukkamala, R.R., Slaats, T., Zanitti, F.: Contracts for cross-organizational workflows as timed dynamic condition response graphs. J. Log. Algebr. Program. **82**(5–7), 164–185 (2013)
4. Schönig, S., Ackermann, L., Jablonski, S.: Towards an implementation of data and resource patterns in constraint-based process models. In: Modelsward, pp. 271–278 (2018)
5. Zeising, M., Schönig, S., Jablonski, S.: Towards a common platform for the support of routine and agile business processes. In: Collaborative Computing: Networking, Applications and Worksharing (2014)
6. Maggi, F.M., Mooij, A., van der Aalst, W.: User-guided discovery of declarative process models. In: CIDM, pp. 192–199 (2011)
7. De Smedt, J., Weerdt, J., Vanthienen, J., Poels, G.: Mixed-paradigm process modeling with intertwined state spaces. Bus. Inf. Syst. Eng. **58**, 12 (2015)
8. Pesic, M., van der Aalst, W.M.P.: A declarative approach for flexible business processes management. In: Eder, J., Dustdar, S. (eds.) BPM 2006. LNCS, vol. 4103, pp. 169–180. Springer, Heidelberg (2006). https://doi.org/10.1007/11837862_18
9. Baier, C., Katoen, J.-P.: Principles of Model Checking. Representation and Mind Series. The MIT Press, Cambridge (2008)
10. Emerson, E.A.: Temporal and modal logic. In: Formal Models and Semantics, pp. 995–1072. Elsevier (1990)
11. Fornara, N., Colombetti, M.: Specifying artificial institutions in the event calculus. In: Handbook of Research on Multi-agent Systems: Semantics and Dynamics of Organizational Models, pp. 335–366. IGI Global (2009)
12. Pesic, M., Schonenberg, H., Van der Aalst, W.M.: Declare: full support for loosely-structured processes. In: 11th IEEE International Enterprise Distributed Object Computing Conference (EDOC 2007), p. 287. IEEE (2007)

13. Bernardi, M.L., Cimitile, M., Di Francescomarino, C., Maggi, F.M.: Using discriminative rule mining to discover declarative process models with non-atomic activities. In: Bikakis, A., Fodor, P., Roman, D. (eds.) RuleML 2014. LNCS, vol. 8620, pp. 281–295. Springer, Cham (2014). https://doi.org/10.1007/978-3-319-09870-8_21

14. Baumann, M., Baumann, M.H., Schönig, S., Jablonski, S.: Resource-aware process model similarity matching. In: ICSOC 2014 Workshops, pp. 96–107 (2014)

15. Lamma, E., Mello, P., Riguzzi, F., Storari, S.: Applying inductive logic programming to process mining. In: Inductive Logic Programming, pp. 132–146 (2007)

16. Chesani, F., Lamma, E., Mello, P., Montali, M., Riguzzi, F., Storari, S.: Exploiting inductive logic programming techniques for declarative process mining. In: Jensen, K., van der Aalst, W.M.P. (eds.) Transactions on Petri Nets and Other Models of Concurrency II. LNCS, vol. 5460, pp. 278–295. Springer, Heidelberg (2009). https://doi.org/10.1007/978-3-642-00899-3_16

17. Westergaard, M., Maggi, F.M.: Looking into the future: using timed automata to provide a priori advice about timed declarative process models. In: Meersman, R., et al. (eds.) OTM 2012, Part I. LNCS, vol. 7565, pp. 250–267. Springer, Heidelberg (2012). https://doi.org/10.1007/978-3-642-33606-5_16

18. Montali, M., Chesani, F., Mello, P., Maggi, F.M.: Towards data-aware constraints in declare. In: SAC, pp. 1391–1396. ACM (2013)

19. Burattin, A., Maggi, F.M., Sperduti, A.: Conformance checking based on multi-perspective declarative process models. Expert Syst. Appl. 65, 194–211 (2016)

20. Schönig, S., Di Ciccio, C., Maggi, F.M., Mendling, J.: Discovery of multi-perspective declarative process models. In: Sheng, Q.Z., Stroulia, E., Tata, S., Bhiri, S. (eds.) ICSOC 2016. LNCS, vol. 9936, pp. 87–103. Springer, Cham (2016). https://doi.org/10.1007/978-3-319-46295-0_6

21. Ackermann, L., Schönig, S., Jablonski, S.: Simulation of multi-perspective declarative process models. In: Dumas, M., Fantinato, M. (eds.) BPM 2016. LNBIP, vol. 281, pp. 61–73. Springer, Cham (2017). https://doi.org/10.1007/978-3-319-58457-7_5

22. Skydanienko, V., Francescomarino, C.D., Maggi, F.: A tool for generating event logs from multi-perspective declare models. In: BPM (Demos) (2018)

23. Ackermann, L., Schönig, S., Petter, S., Schützenmeier, N., Jablonski, S.: Execution of multi-perspective declarative process models. In: OTM 2018 Conferences, pp. 154–172 (2018)

24. van der Aalst, W., Pesic, M., Schonenberg, H.: Declarative workflows: balancing between flexibility and support. In: CSRD, pp. 99–113 (2009)

25. Montali, M., Pesic, M., van der Aalst, W.M.P., Chesani, F., Mello, P., Storari, S.: Declarative specification and verification of service choreographies. ACM Trans. Web 4(1), 3 (2010)

26. Burattin, A., Maggi, F.M., van der Aalst, W.M., Sperduti, A.: Techniques for a posteriori analysis of declarative processes. In: EDOC, Beijing, pp. 41–50. IEEE, September 2012

27. Latvala, T., Biere, A., Heljanko, K., Junttila, T.: Simple bounded LTL model checking. In: Hu, A.J., Martin, A.K. (eds.) FMCAD 2004. LNCS, vol. 3312, pp. 186–200. Springer, Heidelberg (2004). https://doi.org/10.1007/978-3-540-30494-4_14

28. Tauriainen, H.: Automata and linear temporal logic: translations with transition-based acceptance, January 2006

29. Namjoshi, K.S.: An efficiently checkable, proof-based formulation of vacuity in model checking. In: Alur, R., Peled, D.A. (eds.) CAV 2004. LNCS, vol. 3114, pp. 57–69. Springer, Heidelberg (2004). https://doi.org/10.1007/978-3-540-27813-9_5
30. Knuth, D.E., Morris, J.H., Pratt, V.R.: Fast pattern matching in strings. SIAM J. Comput. **6**, 323–350 (1977)

Measures of Quality in Business Process Modeling

Josef Pavlicek[1]([✉]), Petra Pavlickova[1], and Pavel Naplava[2]

[1] Faculty of Information Technology, CTU, Zikova 4, Prague 6 - Dejvice,
166 27 Prague, Czech Republic
{josef.pavlicek,petra.pavlickova}@fit.cvut.cz
[2] Faculty of Electrical Engineering, CTU, Technicka 2, Prague 6 - Dejvice,
166 27 Prague, Czech Republic
pavel.naplava@fel.cvut.cz

Abstract. Business process modeling is undoubtedly one of the most important parts of Applied (Business) Informatics. Quality of business process models (diagrams) is crucial for any purpose in this area. The goal of a process analyst's work is to create generally understandable, explicit, unambiguous and error-free models. If a process is properly described, created models can be used as an input into deep analysis and optimization. Optimization is mostly focused on a higher efficiency of the process or at least on a better clarification of its meaning and working. Objective: It can be assumed that properly designed business process models (similarly as in the case of correctly written algorithms) contain characteristics that can be mathematically described. If it is possible to find measurable attributes of business process model's quality, it will be possible to define a different quality maturity levels of business process modeling results. Furthermore, it will be possible creating a tool helping process analysts designing proper models. Method: A systematic literature review was conducted in order to find and analyze business process model's design and business process model's quality measuring methods. Results: It was found that mentioned area had already been subject of research investigation in the past. Thirty-three suitable scientific publications and twenty-two quality measures were found. Conclusions: Analyzed articles and existing quality measures do not reflect all important attributes of business process model's clarity, simplicity and completeness. Therefore it would be appropriate adding new measures of quality.

Keywords: Business process modeling · Business processes · Measures of quality · BPMN

1 Introduction

A project of business processes modeling has been running at the Czech Technical University in Prague at Faculty of Electrical Engineering (CTU FEE) since 2009 (led by the Centre for Knowledge Management [1, 2]). Within this project more than 400 business processes in BPMN notation have described. Identical projects (also led by

© Springer Nature Switzerland AG 2019
R. Pergl et al. (Eds.): EOMAS 2019, LNBIP 366, pp. 146–155, 2019.
https://doi.org/10.1007/978-3-030-35646-0_11

the Centre for Knowledge Management) has been implemented at CTU - Faculty of Mechanical Engineering, University Centre for Energy Efficient Buildings, University of West Bohemia and Škoda Praha. An increasing demand for the future can be expected for business process modeling not only in academic, but also in commercial environment It was empirically encountered various difficulties which stem from deficiencies BPMN during all mentioned projects [3]. These were mainly:

- Widely varying levels of detail captured business processes among individual creators.
- Changing participant's role during the execution of one business process.
- The high number of BPMN symbols (tasks, gateways, events, etc.) within a business process.
- Multiplicity of same BPMN symbols.
- The different levels of the distribution of one business process into multiple sub processes.

The above-mentioned shortcomings have often led to a redesign of the entire business process. Therefore, the time required for quality of design and process description was disproportionately increased, which should be simple, easy to understand, and above all to clearly demonstrate real execution, including all details.

The goal of this study is to provide a systematic search of the available literature and to find answers to the following questions:

1. Can the quality of business process models be measured using certain measures, indicators or other methods?
2. Do any measures, indicators or methods exist?
3. If so, are they used in common practice?
4. If so, are they part of any standards?
5. Is there any standard for presenting business process models?

The meaningfulness of mentioned questions confirms one publication [5] where the authors deal with similar problems of measuring the quality and effectiveness of ten thousand processes. For this reason, we decided to arrange for a systematic literature review in order to find and analyze primary studies about business process modeling and measures of business process design quality.

2 Research Method

2.1 Search Process

Systematic literature review was performed on the basis of [4]. To ensure quality, we sought sources in knowledgeable digital libraries. We used the following databases:

- Web of Science
- ACM Digital Library
- EBSCO
- IEEE Xplore

- Scopus
- SpringerLink.

The area in which we wanted to perform literature review was the one of process measures. When we were searching for relevant resources we started from general keywords such as "Process metrics" and "BPMN measures". The granularity of the search was gradually improved by refinement of the keywords. The final form of keywords stuck at "Process quality metrics" and "Process complexity metrics". Using these keywords we found set of relevant resources. In the last step of the search we were able to specify process metrics using these expressions:

- Process coupling complexity.
- Process cohesion complexity.
- Control flow complexity.

We have also influenced the results of our research by following criteria:

- Publications are available online, in full text.
- Language of publications was limited to English.
- Publications are cited in other publications.
- Publications take the form of scientific work, books or conference publications.

The results of the search were generated in the period from 22nd January 2015 to 24th February 2015 and contains the literary sources published by this date.

3   Results

3.1   Search Results, Data Extraction and Synthesis

During literature reviews we found Thirty-three suitable scientific publications [6–37]. We read each of these publications and selected information regarding to measures of quality in business processes. Subsequently we found twenty-two measures of quality. The results of the study sources can be assessed as very relevant and of high-quality. We searched relevant publications only in the established digital libraries. We therefore conclude that the quality of the studies is high.

3.2   Measures of Quality

As mentioned above we found twenty-two measures of quality:

1.   Number of activities (NOA, NOT) - [5, 8, 10, 11, 19, 20, 30, 32, 35].
2.   Control-Flow Complexity (CFC) - [5, 7, 8, 10, 11, 14–17, 19–22, 25, 27, 29–33, 35, 37].
3.   Max/mean nesting depth - [19, 20, 32].
4.   Number of handles - [19].

5. Cognitive weight (Cognitive Complexity) - [9, 13, 19, 20, 32, 35].
6. BPM (Anti) Patterns - [19, 20].
7. Fan-in/Fan-out (Modularization) - [11, 19, 20, 35].
8. Coefficient of network complexity (CNC) - [5, 8, 10, 11, 14, 26, 30, 32].
9. Cyclomatic number - [14, 21, 26].
10. Complexity index (CI) - [5, 8, 14, 26].
11. Restrictiveness estimator (RT) - [8, 14, 26].
12. Number of trees in graph - [14, 26].
13. Process Cohesion (TPC, LPC) - [6, 18, 24, 33].
14. Process Coupling (CBO, RFC, MPC, ICP) - [18, 23, 24, 33].
15. Process coupling/cohesion ratio - [18, 24].
16. Halstead-based Process Complexity (HPC) - [8, 10, 11, 25, 32, 33, 35].
17. Interface Complexity (IC) - [8, 10, 11, 32–35].
18. Density - [36].
19. Cross-Connectivity (CC) - [10, 29, 36].
20. CP - [12].
21. GQM - [20].
22. Q0, Q1, Q3 - [28].

The frequency of occurrence of metrics in publications is shown in Fig. 1. The most widely accepted metrics are (1) the Control-Flow Complexity, (2) number of Activities and (3) coefficient of network Complexity.

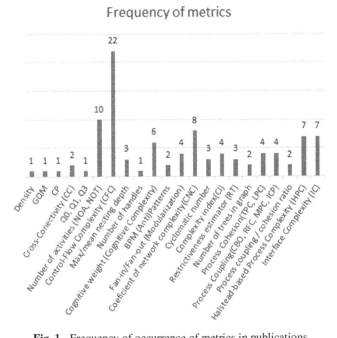

Fig. 1. Frequency of occurrence of metrics in publications.

In terms of time we found publications between 2001 and 2014. Only one publication has earlier publication date as specified in Fig. 2. Figure 2 shows that the interest in metrics increased in 2005. Most publications were appearing between 2006 and 2010.

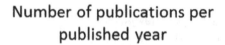

Number of publications per published year

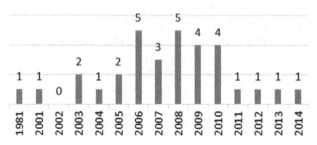

Fig. 2. Number of publications per published year.

3.3 Demographic Data

From a demographic point of view we found out that publications come mostly from Western European regions, which indicates an increased interest in this issue, particularly in countries like the Netherlands and Portugal (Fig. 3).

Number of publications per state

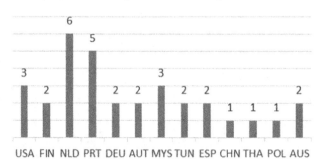

Fig. 3. Number of publications per state.

3.4 Metrics Implementation

We developed "**Metrics calculation software**" [40] according to the presented results. The first version of this software was presented on the EOMAS 2016. From the year 2016 till end of year 2018 we updated the software calculation methods according to our research [41, 42]. This software is available for free. The software is running in the application server [41]. The approach for that is via an internet browser. It is not necessary to install any software into the computer.

4   Discussion

From the research it is obvious that similar problems are solved by other scientific teams. As we supposed, a lot of metrics are based on the BPM chart analysis. Typical examples can be: Number of activities, Control-Flow Complexity etc. The metrics based on the chart analysis have got deep background in the typical software metrics as: Cyclomatic number, etc. [14, 21, 26].

It is not easy to use these metrics in the real business at all, because the BPM is influenced by factors which cannot be found from the BPM chart only. These factors influence the final business process indirectly.

For example, these factors can be identified according to the actor type used in the BPM [38, 39]:

- Exactly defined actor (for example students).
- Fuzzy defined actor (for example study department – nobody knows who will serve study requests – it is ambiguous).
- Black box actor type (for example another system which communicates by defined interface with the final business process).

Other factors can be identified according to the BPM development team skills:

- Beginners (less than 50 models designed).
- Intermediate (less than 500 models designed).
- Excellent (more than 500 models designed).

And finally, other factors that can be identified according to the BPM requested company organization type [38, 39]:

1. Organic (organization with excellent knowledge sharing).
2. Semi-detached (organization with mixed quality knowledge sharing).
3. Embedded (organization with problematic knowledge sharing).

In fact the current BPM metrics do not take example from COCOMO [38] and other methodologies (Function points, Use Case points). These methodologies try to describe the implementation process more comprehensively. In the Constructive cost model COCOMO [38], the authors defined cost estimation for the software development. Although the business process modeling is not software development, we can recognize some parallels. The parallels are factors which we have defined above. These factors can influence process modeling significantly. We can supposed to find more factors influencing the BPM.

The COCOMO [38] defines function count by type, direct quotation:

"The unadjusted function counts should be counted by a lead technical person based on information in the software requirements and documents design. The number of each of the five user function types should be counted (Internal Logical File* (ILF), External Interface File (EIF), External Input (EI), External Output (EO), and External Inquiry

(EQ))." (Fig. 4), [38]. The COCOMO determines the complexity level for function counts, direct quotation:

"*Classify each function count into Low, Average and High complexity levels depending upon the number of data element types contained and the number of file types referenced. Use the following scheme*" [38].

For ILF and EIF				For EO and EQ				For EI			
Record Elements	Data Elements			File Types	Data Elements			File Types	Data Elements		
	1 - 19	20 - 50	51+		1 - 5	6 - 19	20+		1 - 4	5 - 15	16+
1	Low	Low	Avg	0 or 1	Low	Low	Avg	0 or 1	Low	Low	Avg
2 - 5	Low	Avg	High	2 - 3	Low	Avg	High	2 - 3	Low	Avg	High
6+	Avg	High	High	4+	Avg	High	High	3+	Avg	High	High

Fig. 4. Determined function counts by type COCOMO example [38].

Based on the COCOMO approaches we can try to understand the business process as a chain of activities (parallel with COCOMO functions).

5 Conclusion

From this point of view, it's very useful to design more business process metrics based on the factors of realization. Not only based on the BPM chart analysis.

There are examples which we found during the research:

- Actor role is changed twice during the process of applicant study to student. It should be solved by two actors – Applicant and Student. These roles may follow, but do not change from one to the other.
- The fuzzy actor responsibility. The typical example is if some important artefact for the process (for example the invoice) is consumed by the exact actor (director of accounting department) or the fuzzy actor (accounting department).
- The business process is joined with more processes that can be wrong or ineffective. In this case the business process can be designed perfectly and quality metrics can report very positive values, nevertheless the complete system will not be working effectively.

All these examples cannot be described by the metrics based on the BPM chart analysis. Similarly as the COCOMO uses attributes of function complexity, we should try to design new attributes for process complexity from the point of realization. Today we can suppose the process model designer skills are fundamental. Do we have high or low skills with modeling processes? These factors are described and used for software complexity prediction by COCOMO. Maybe it will be useful to define them for the BPM, too. This questions are still waiting for the answer. To start finding the answer for them, we developed software tool. All metrics presented in this paper are now covered via **Metrics calculation software** [40]. We worked on that from 2016 till now. We try to get interested person for some easy way to measure his/her BPM model. The volunteers are helping us to update implemented metrics. The problem is, the calculation algorithm that must be robust. The BPM cases are not generating identical output during the model saving. Thanks to that, we need to make a lot of updates at the software. And in need time.   .

References

1. Hronza, R., Špeta, M.: Business Process Center of Excellence at the Faculty of Electrical Engineering at the Czech Technical University in Prague. In: 2013 IEEE 15th Conference on Business Informatics, pp. 346–349 (2013)
2. Pavel, N., Radek, H., Jan, K., Josef, P.: How to successfully start the transformation of an academic institution. Case study on the process mapping project at the Czech Technical University. In: Complementary proceedings of the 8th Workshop on Transformation & Engineering of Enterprises (TEE 2014), and the 1st International Workshop on Capability-oriented Business Informatics (CoBI 2014) co-located with the 16th IEEE International Conference on B, pp. 1–15 (2014)
3. Van Nuffel, D., Mulder, H., Van Kervel, S.: Enhancing the formal foundations of BPMN by enterprise ontology. In: Albani, A., Barjis, J., Dietz, J.L.G. (eds.) CIAO!/EOMAS. LNBIP, vol. 34, pp. 115–129. Springer, Heidelberg (2009). https://doi.org/10.1007/978-3-642-01915-9_9
4. Kitchenham, B., Charters, S.: Guidelines for performing Systematic Literature Reviews in Software Engineering (2007)
5. Vanderfeesten, I., Cardoso, J., Mendling, J., Reijers, H.A., Van Der Aalst, W.: Quality metrics for business process models. In: BPM and Workflow Handbook, pp. 1–12 (2007)
6. Reijers, H.A.: A cohesion metric for the definition of activities in a workflow process. In: Proceedings EMMSAD (2003). http://www.win.tue.nl/~hreijers/H.A.ReijersBestanden/metric.pdf. Accessed 01 Feb 2015
7. Fu, X., Zou, P., Ma, Y., Jiang, Y., Yue, K.: A control-flow complexity measure of web service composition process. In: Proceedings of 2010 IEEE Asia-Pacific Services Computing Conference, APSCC 2010, pp. 712–716 (2010)
8. Cardoso, J., Mendling, J., Neumann, G., Reijers, H.A.: A discourse on complexity of process models. In: Eder, J., Dustdar, S. (eds.) BPM 2006. LNCS, vol. 4103, pp. 117–128. Springer, Heidelberg (2006). https://doi.org/10.1007/11837862_13
9. Shao, J., Wang, Y.: A new measure of software complexity based on cognitive weights "Une nouvelle métrique de complexité logicielle basée sur les poids cognitifs," October, vol. 28, no. 2, pp. 69–74 (2003)
10. Muketha, G.M., Abd Ghani, A.A., Selamat, M.H., Atan, R.: A survey of business process complexity metrics. Inf. Technol. J. 9, 1336–1344 (2010)
11. Makni, L., Khlif, W., Haddar, N.Z., Ben-abdallah, H.: A tool for evaluating the quality of business process models overview on current metrics for BPM, pp. 230–242
12. Vanderfeesten, I., Cardoso, J., Reijers, H.A.: A weighted coupling metric for business process models. In: CEUR Workshop Proceedings, vol. 247, pp. 41–44 (2007)
13. Gruhn, V., Laue, R.: Adopting the cognitive complexity measure for business process models. In: 2006 5th IEEE International Conference on Cognitive Informatics, vol. 1, pp. 236–241 (2006)
14. Roy, S., Sajeev, A.S.M., Bihary, S., Ranjan, A.: An empirical study of error patterns in industrial business process models. IEEE Trans. Serv. Comput. 7(2), 140–153 (2014)
15. Parizi, R.M., Ghani, A.A.A.: An ensemble of complexity metrics for BPEL web processes. In: Proceedings of 9th ACIS International Conference on Software Engineering, Artificial Intelligence, Networking, and Parallel/Distributed Computing. SNPD 2008 2nd Int. Work. Adv. Internet Technol. Appl., pp. 753–758 (2008)

16. Rolón, E., Cardoso, J., García, F., Ruiz, F., Piattini, M.: Analysis and validation of control-flow complexity measures with BPMN process models. In: Halpin, T., et al. (eds.) BPMDS/EMMSAD. LNBIP, vol. 29, pp. 58–70. Springer, Heidelberg (2009). https://doi.org/10.1007/978-3-642-01862-6_6

17. Cardoso, J.: Business process control-flow complexity: metric, evaluation, and validation. Int. J. Web Serv. Res. **5**, 49–76 (2008)

18. Reijers, H.A., Vanderfeesten, Irene T.P.: Cohesion and coupling metrics for workflow process design. In: Desel, J., Pernici, B., Weske, M. (eds.) BPM 2004. LNCS, vol. 3080, pp. 290–305. Springer, Heidelberg (2004). https://doi.org/10.1007/978-3-540-25970-1_19. http://www.processmining.org/_media/publications/reijers2004.pdf. Accessed 01 Feb 2015

19. Gruhn, V., Laue, R.: Complexity metrics for business process models. In: 9th International Conference on Business Information Systems, pp. 1–12 (2006)

20. Azim, A., Ghani, A., Tieng, K., Geoffrey, W., Muketha, M., Wen, W.P.: Complexity metrics for measuring the understandability and maintainability of business process models using goal-question-metric (GQM). J. Comput. Sci. **8**(5), 219–225 (2008)

21. Lassen, K.B., van der Aalst, W.M.P.: Complexity metrics for Workflow nets. Inf. Softw. Technol. **51**(3), 610–626 (2009)

22. Cardoso, J.: Control-flow complexity measurement of processes and Weyuker's properties. In: 6th International Conference on Enformatika, vol. 8, no. 8, pp. 213–218 (2005)

23. Khlif, W., Zaaboub, N., Ben-Abdallah, H.: Coupling metrics for business process modeling. WSEAS Trans. Comput. **9**, 31–41 (2010)

24. Vanderfeesten, I., Reijers, H.A., van der Aalst, W.M.P.: Evaluating workflow process designs using cohesion and coupling metrics. Comput. Ind. **59**, 420–437 (2008)

25. Solichah, I., Hamilton, M., Mursanto, P., Ryan, C., Perepletchikov, M.: Exploration on software complexity metrics for business process model and notation. In: 2013 International Conference on Advanced Computer Science and Information Systems, pp. 31–37 (2013)

26. Latva-Koivisto, A.M.: Finding a complexity measure for business process models. Complexity (2001). http://citeseerx.ist.psu.edu/viewdoc/download?doi=10.1.1.25.2991&rep=rep1&type=pdf. Accessed 01 Feb 2015

27. Cardoso, J.: How to measure the control-flow complexity of web process and workflows. In: Workflow Handbook 2005, pp. 199–212 (2005)

28. Huang, Z., Kumar, A.: New quality metrics for evaluating process models. In: Ardagna, D., Mecella, M., Yang, J. (eds.) BPM 2008. LNBIP, vol. 17, pp. 164–170. Springer, Heidelberg (2009). https://doi.org/10.1007/978-3-642-00328-8_16

29. Vanderfeesten, I., Reijers, H.A., Mendling, J., van der Aalst, W.M.P., Cardoso, J.: On a quest for good process models: the cross-connectivity metric. In: Bellahsène, Z., Léonard, M. (eds.) CAiSE 2008. LNCS, vol. 5074, pp. 480–494. Springer, Heidelberg (2008). https://doi.org/10.1007/978-3-540-69534-9_36

30. Mendling, J., Neumann, G., Van Der Aalst, W.M.P.: On the correlation between process model metrics and errors. In: 26th International Conference on Conceptual Modeling, pp. 173–178 (2007)

31. Cardoso, J.: Process control-flow complexity metric: an empirical validation. In: Proceedings - 2006 IEEE International Conference on Services Computing, SCC 2006, pp. 167–173 (2006)

32. Kluza, K., Nalepa, G.J.: Proposal of square metrics for measuring business process model complexity. In: Federated Conference on Computer Science and Information Systems, pp. 919–922 (2012)

33. Khlif, W., Makni, L.: Quality metrics for business process modeling. In: Proceedings of the 9th WSEAS International Conference on Applied Computer Science, vol. 9, no. 1, pp. 195–200 (2009)

34. Henry, S., Kafura, D.: Software structure metrics based on information flow. IEEE Trans. Softw. Eng. **SE-7**(5), 510–518 (1981)

35. Thammarak, K.: Survey complexity metrics for reusable business process. In: National Conference on Applied Computer Technology and Information System, pp. 18–22 (2010)

36. Mendling, J.: Testing density as a complexity metric for EPCs. In: Analysis (2006)

37. Sánchez-González, L., Ruiz, F., García, F., Cardoso, J.: Towards thresholds of control flow complexity measures for BPMN models. In: Proceedings of the 2011 ACM Symposium on Applied Computing, pp. 1445–1450 (2011)

38. Boehm, B., Clark, B., Horowitz, E., Westland, Ch., Madachy, R., Selby, R.: Cost models for future software life cycle processes: COCOMO 2.0. Ann. Softw. Eng. 1(1), 57–94 (1995)

39. Pavlicek, J.: The estimation of managerial characteristics of IS development in the stage of requirements specification, Pavlicek Ph.D. work, CULS-2006

40. Pavlicek, J., Hronza, R., Pavlickova, P.: Educational business process model skills improvement. In: Pergl, R., Molhanec, M., Babkin, E., Fosso Wamba, S. (eds.) EOMAS 2016. LNBIP, vol. 272, pp. 172–184. Springer, Cham (2016). https://doi.org/10.1007/978-3-319-49454-8_12. ISBN 978-3-319-49454-8

41. Pavlicek, J., Hronza, R., Pavlickova, P., Jelinkova, K.: The business process model quality metrics. In: Pergl, R., Lock, R., Babkin, E., Molhanec, M. (eds.) EOMAS 2017, vol. 298, pp. 134–148. Springer, Cham (2017). https://doi.org/10.1007/978-3-319-68185-6_10. ISBN 978-3-319-681849

42. Pavlicek, J., Pavlickova, P.: Methods for evaluating the quality of process modelling tools. In: Pergl, R., Babkin, E., Lock, R., Malyzhenkov, P., Merunka, V. (eds.) EOMAS 2018. LNBIP, vol. 332, pp. 171–177. Springer, Cham (2018). https://doi.org/10.1007/978-3-030-00787-4_12. ISBN 978-3-030-00787-4

Performance Impact to the Applying Design Patternization Techniques to Object-Relational Databases

Boris Schegolev[1]($\boxtimes$), Himesha Wijekoon[1], Jakub Štěpán Novák[2], and Vojtěch Merunka[1,3]

[1] Faculty of Economics and Management, Department of Information Engineering, Czech University of Life Sciences Prague, Prague, Czech Republic
{schegolev,wijekoon,merunka}@pef.czu.cz,
vojtech.merunka@fjfi.cvut.cz
[2] Faculty of Economics and Management, Department of Information Technology, Czech University of Life Sciences Prague, Prague, Czech Republic
novakjakub_stepan@pef.czu.cz
[3] Faculty of Nuclear Sciences and Physical Engineering, Department of Software Engineering, Czech Technical University in Prague, Prague, Czech Republic

Abstract. This paper looks at performance aspects of applying object-oriented design patterns to databases mainly on the level of computational complexity. Considering selected patterns that may be applied on both application and database layer, algorithm complexity is evaluated. The authors focus on purely theoretical computational complexity of given algorithms and presents our preliminary research in this area which tries to be independent on individual database vendors and their particular implementations leading to a simple apple-to-apple comparison of the performance impact to the applying of the given patternization technique.

Keywords: Object-oriented database · Relational database · Database performance · Execution complexity · Design patterns

1 Introduction

Object orientation is considered one of the most important paradigms in software engineering in the last several decades. It came with an important advancement in the form of wide application of design patterns to support chosen solutions. With the object-related support in the databases, it became possible to transfer object-oriented models into databases including translation of corresponding design patterns and their reimplementation on database layer.

Unfortunately, after the initial hopes of the 1990s (as written in [2, 11] and similar books from that time), we still do not have a wide use of object-oriented databases and the use of object-oriented design patterns has proven to be rather a complication than a benefit. Great progress has been made in the field of the object-oriented theory (for example [1]), but all the new advantages of the object-oriented approach are based on behavioral and functional features, making them very little usable in database technology.

© Springer Nature Switzerland AG 2019
R. Pergl et al. (Eds.): EOMAS 2019, LNBIP 366, pp. 156–163, 2019.
https://doi.org/10.1007/978-3-030-35646-0_12

2   Motivation

Database technology was always led by the effort to meet the requirements imposed by practical applications. Today, the most used programming paradigm on the client-side of database systems is the object orientation for many positive reasons. However, at the server-side still remain a relational database. Of course, there is some remarkable tendency to extend the relational database with various functions, for example, the possibility of direct representation of complex data types or return to the network-like (e.g. graph) database model with direct pointers among database records but the old prognoses did not come true.

Current systems integrate the database technology with the object-oriented paradigm which was developed in the area of programming languages and graphical user interfaces. This trend is driven by industrial development even though there are not yet strong and consolidated theoretical foundations for database design. Although, from a technical point of view, an object-oriented database is a return back to network databases and/or graph databases that have been known and used since the 1960s, the theoretical tools for their design do not use the experience of that time, but only object-oriented application programming which are, however, useful only for constructing software running in memory and not automatically applicable with the same positive effect in large data collections on disks and multiuser and transactional data processing modes.

However, also the pure object-oriented databases are not a suitable environment for applying object-design patterns. This is due to the fact that object-oriented programming design patterns assume that objects are stored in the random access memory (RAM) with direct pointer access, just as it is in object-oriented application programming languages. But object-oriented databases have a different memory model (derived from network and graph databases) and cannot use the benefit from placing all their objects in the standard RAM. In addition, databases have large datasets where we need to search objects using their different attribute values which are dynamically calculated just because of design patterns and cannot be easily indexed. We believe that this is the reason for the remaining small practical usage of pure object-oriented databases and, on the contrary, the popularity of a hybrid model with object-oriented client having data in a relational database server using some object-relational interface. But even this hybrid solution does not help to solve design pattern problems.

3   Object-Relational Performance

Mapping between client-side objects and serve-side records in relational tables is a well-known weak point of most practical database applications [12]. Although pure object databases allow objects to be stored directly on the server without transformation, but with the above reasons, this solution does not bring any significant increase in performance. We only get good results here when the object database just emulates the static graph of interconnected records as we used it in network databases from the past [13].

3.1 Language Call Complexity

Measuring algorithmic complexity in procedural languages is well defined. Also, there are known theoretical complexities for common data structures. For description of such complexities Bachman's and Landau's Big O notation is used. In the context of this paper, it is important to understand that Big O is most relevant to working with large collection of data and is used to classify algorithms according to how their running time (and also memory space usage) grow with the size of input collection [3, 9].

Another thing is that the complexity of individual language calls (going through the current language statement to the next one, i.e. cyclomatic complexity) is may be easily identified when working with procedural languages. Databases focus on collection-wide operations, so Big O provides a better overview of how demanding given changes may be.

3.2 Execution Plan

Execution plan generated for a given query in a database depends largely on the specific optimization technique implemented by the given vendor. Furthermore, execution plans rely on cost-based optimization, which leads to an approximation of a real performance impact into the database, that are also vendor-dependent [4]. For purposes of this paper, a theoretical computational complexity has to be formulated so that there can be found a simple apple-to-apple comparison of the performance impact.

4 Object Patterns in Databases

Reference to application of object-oriented patterns to non object-oriented databases is somewhat remote. This is due to the fact that SQL-based databases do not provide direct support for class definition and instantiation. A certain level of abstraction is required to make application of certain groups of patterns possible on a relational database management system (RDBMS) directly.

In application context it may be assumed that application-level business objects are mapped to tabular structures of SQL databases. Generally speaking, entities correspond to classes. This also translates applied structural and behavioral patterns to the database layer. We may further assume that selected object-oriented patterns are generally applicable in database context.

4.1 Adapter/Bridge

What it is in Object World. Converts the interface of a class into another interface clients expect [7]. Implementation of these patterns lets classes work together that couldn't otherwise because of incompatible interfaces. These patterns are demonstrated in Figs. 1 and 2 respectively.

What it is in Database World. Adapter/Bridge patterns may be implemented as a functional call over individual rows or returned values. For conformity, the result may be wrapped in a view or a procedure output.

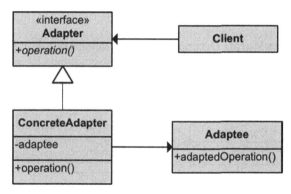

Fig. 1. Adapter

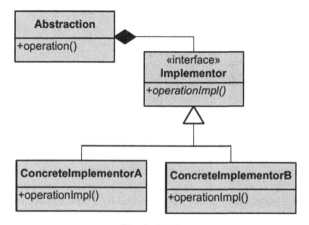

Fig. 2. Bridge

Processing of functional calls over individual rows/values are rather slow. They may not be cached or indexed or otherwise optimized.

Complexity. Assuming there are no queries going back into the same table within the functional call, it is safe to say that the computational complexity remains same: $O(n)$ for sequential search and $O(log_b(n))$ for indexed search, where b is the basis of logarithm and n is the size of collection. For a typical b-tree index, this is about 5. It also needs to be stated that in case a search is happening on the result value, usage of index to retrieve the value is effectively prevented. Thus, even for indexed columns the algorithmic complexity stays linear computational complexity $O(n)$.

The different issue is that in the real world there are multiple other factors that come into consideration. For example, memory requirements to run per-row calculations may also become an issue, as in the cases considered here all processes happen within a single transaction.

4.2 Decorator

What it is in Object World. Decorator attaches additional responsibilities to an object dynamically [8]. This provides a flexible alternative to sub-classing for extending functionality. Decorator pattern is illustrated in Fig. 3.

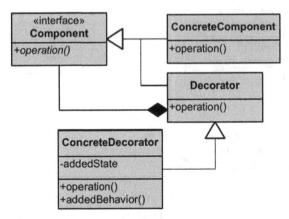

Fig. 3. Decorator

What it is in Database World. The implementation of this design pattern is done by simply JOINing individual data collections into larger blocks for behavioral extension.

If we consider a normalized relationship defined by a numeric key reference, we end up with an index-based search or a nested loop.

Complexity. The join complexity depends on the algorithm used, which further depends on statistics and index availability. It is generally considered to be between the best possible value of $O(1)$ for the ideal hash joins, $O(log_b(n))$ for index loops and $O(n)$ for only sequence scans.

Technically, the concept of unifying different classes for extended functionality is one of the things RDBMS were specifically designed for. For simple cases of class use in context of the *Decorator* pattern the efficiency is very high and requires no further fine-tuning. Of course, in cases of awkward design, the composition may build on another composition, degrading the performance near to $O(n)$.

4.3 Observer

What it is in Object World. Observer defines a one-to-many dependency between objects so that when one object changes state, all its dependents are notified and updated automatically [7]. This pattern is depicted in Fig. 4.

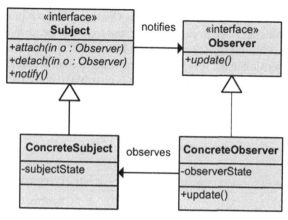

Fig. 4. Observer

What it is in Database World. Here we intentionally skip the notify-listen approach provided by some RDBMS vendors [6]. This is because the notification system does not handle collections as classes in OOP understanding, thus rendering the matching of individual points between OOP and database implementations impossible.

Alternatively, given concept is achieved through assigning triggers to data collections. The minor difference in understanding is that SQL natively works with collections (classes) and processing individual entities is done with application of filtering conditions on processing instructions.

Complexity. The semantic approach to implementation of the Observer pattern largely resembles the concept used in case of Adapter/Bridge patterns. In both described situations individual rows require further functional calls per individual instance (row being processed). In this case though, the algorithm may not be optimized to use better than $O(n)$ complexity due to the fact that every individual value is being forwarded to the functional call.

5 Discussion

It has been shown that some object-oriented patterns may be translated to databases. We recognized that performance impact differs from one pattern to another. Performance may be measured using standard tools and notations, so application of a pattern, too. We used a limited tool set (Big O notation), yet other complexity estimates may further refine the results.

Based on our analysis, we can assemble a list of database-friendly design patterns. The main criterion will be their influence on computational complexity, which cannot be worse than logarithmic. A worse-than-logarithmic patterns should not be used because they invoke too long computational time when used in large collection of data. The important question remains if such patterns should be generally avoided or replaced with something else. The example of these patterns is *Observer*. It is our practice to limit the use of triggers particularly due to performance reasons. Another example of database-unfriendly pattern is *Adapter/Bridge* which can be updated to store *lazy initialized data* (e.g. creation and writing in the first time when it is needed) in multiple forms, so that a different projection replaces a functional call. It is possible to make the same functional call, store the result as a new column, and then provide different "views" on the same data set. The results are summarized in Table 1.

Table 1. The results

	The worse comp. complexity	Is database-friendly	Proposed strategy
Adapter	$O(n)$	No	Replace by multiple lazy initialized data
Bridge	$O(n)$	No	Replace by multiple lazy initialized data
Observer	$O(n)$	No	Avoid usage
Decorator	$O(log_b(n))$	Yes	No need

6   Conclusion

In our text, we have described the cause of the remaining small extension of pure object-oriented databases in practice and the difficulties that programmers have to deal with in the case of a hybrid model consisting of an object-oriented database client and a relational database server.

We believe that the solution must be found not only in the new technical possibilities of object indexing in the object-oriented database systems, but also in the search for new database-friendly object-oriented design patterns.

Our future work will focus on the empirical justification of our statements and the search for new design patterns and validate them in the *GemStone/S v6.7.1* database server environment.

References

1. Abadi, M., Cardelli, L.: A Theory of Objects. Springer, New York (1998)
2. Bertino, E., Martino, L.: Object-Oriented Database Systems. Addison-Wesley, Wokingham (1993)
3. Black, P.E.: Big-O notation. Dictionary of Algorithms and Data Structures. U.S. National Institute of Standards and Technology (2019). https://xlinux.nist.gov/dads/HTML/bigOnotation.html. Accessed 31 Mar 2019
4. Chaudhuri, S.: Query optimizers: time to rethink the contract? In: Binnig, C., Dageville, B. (eds.) Proceedings of the 2009 ACM SIGMOD International Conference on Management of Data (SIGMOD 2009), pp. 961–968. ACM, New York (2009). https://doi.org/10.1145/1559845.1559955

5. Date, C.J.: An Introduction to Database Systems. Addison-Wesley, Reading (1995)
6. Fontaine, D.: Mastering PostgreSQL in Application Development. Lulu.com (2017). ISBN 978-024494525
7. Freeman, E., Freeman, E., Sierra, K., Bates, B.: Head First Design Patterns (paperback), p. 244. O'Reilly Media, Sebastopol (2004). ISBN 978-0-596-00712-6. OCLC 809772256
8. Gamma, E., Helm, R., Johnson, R., Vlissides, J.: Design Patterns: Elements of Reusable Object-Oriented Software with a foreword of Grady BOOCH. Addison-Wesley Professional, Reading (1995). ISBN 978-0201633610
9. Knuth, D.: Chapter 1.2.11: Asymptotic representations. Fundamental algorithms. In: The Art of Computer Programming, vol. 1, 3rd edn. Addison-Wesley, Reading (1997). ISBN 978-0-201-89683-1
10. Gemstone: GemStone/S v6.7.1 Programming Guide, GemStone Systems, Inc. (2018)
11. Loomis, M.: ODBMS vs. relational. J. Object-Oriented Program. **3**, 79–82 (1990)
12. Loomis, M.: Hitting the relational wall. J. Object-Oriented Program. **7**, 56–59 (1994)
13. Taylor, R.W., Frank, R.L.: CODASYL Database Management Systems. ACM Comput. Surv. **8**(1), 67–103 (1976)

Invited Workshop Notes

Business Process Models (BPMN and DEMO Notation) - Usability Study

Petra Pavlickova[✉] and Josef Pavlicek

Faculty of Information Technology, CTU, Zikova 4, Prague 6 - Dejvice,
166 27 Prague, Czech Republic
{Petra.Pavlickova,Josef.Pavlicek}@fit.cvut.cz

Abstract. This paper deals with the comparison of BPMN and DEMO process modelling tools in the form of Usability study. The authors present the methods used to compare, define the appropriate equipment of the laboratory and propose the CASE study model. The results from the two CASE studies performed are critical and define the conclusion. The result is a recommendation when it is advisable to use BPMN and when DEMO. Another result is the proposed method of verification of process modelling tools.

Keywords: BPMN · DEMO · Eye tracking · Usability study · Process modelling tools

1 Introduction

Over the years, our team has addressed a number of issues regarding the quality of process models that have been published at EOMAS [1, 2], but also in journals and scientific articles [3–8]. We discussed the BPMN notation in great detail [9, 10]. Our team has proposed a number of methods to measure and qualitatively verify the quality of process models [3]. We have demonstrated the possibility of using well-known techniques to follow the classical Usability Study method as reported by Jacob Nielsen with his team [15, 16, 21]. In addition to this approach, we suggested using methods published by Josef Pavlíček, Petra Pavlíčková, Radek Hronza etc. [1–3]. Unlike conducting a usability study by Jacob Nielsen, they work with a large number of participants in the study. This principle is called collaborative. We have designed the collaborative title [17] based on experience from a number of studies. These have demonstrated effective interaction between participants during the study.

The classical approach is based on the assumption that the participant is enclosed in the room itself. There is only a moderator in his presence and only if the participant needs some help. Some variations of usability studies allow testing two separate participants at one time. However, the basic assumption of the study lies in the so-called voice thinking. Simply solved, the participant says what they are thinking. This will allow one or two participants to test the task at one time.

The collaborative approach focuses on the interaction of participants with the problem addressed [17]. To achieve this, the environment in which the participants are placed

© Springer Nature Switzerland AG 2019
R. Pergl et al. (Eds.): EOMAS 2019, LNBIP 366, pp. 167–174, 2019.
https://doi.org/10.1007/978-3-030-35646-0_13

must be appropriately oriented. A HUBRU usability laboratory [17] located on CULS is provided for this purpose. These workstations orientation allows us to test a task with up to 10 participants at a time. Two workstations are also equipped with eye tracking tools. This also strengthens the qualitative outcome of the study, where the participants' statements obtained by the final interview are supported by a record of eye movement. In addition, we have also presented this practice last year at the EOMAS 2018 [23]. conference in addition to scientific articles and scientific papers [1–8].

Several interesting effects occur during the study. These can be classified by the following scale:

- **Uncertainty** - originates either in a wrong assignment, or in a lack of participant's mental capacity during a task, or an error in Usability. Uncertainty manifests itself in the effort to cooperate with "copying" from colleagues sitting side by side.
- **Rapture** - The participant is surprised by the GUI response and falls out of concentration. It manifests itself either by voice expression or very often by facial expression.
- **Blocking** - the participant is unable to continue. This is either due to a gross mistake in entering the test scenario, or a manifest violation of the participant's mental model by responding to the graphical interface.
- **Frustration** - its manifestation is loud commenting on the currently solved task.

The participant intuitively awaits cooperation with the environment that "has to have the same problem" (and very often does). There is a heated debate. This is obviously a GUI error (or a totally inappropriate test scenario).

In the case of collaborative testing, we do not evaluate or gradualize these grades. We are wondering whether or not it has occurred. These are in fact absolute scales. If so, it becomes a hypothesis for the researcher. This hypothesis must be confirmed or excluded in interviews with participants.

Furthermore, the collaborative approach allows the study to be conducted using the:

- **Heuristic** - here we monitor whether the participant goes through all steps of the test scenario in the required order and is not disturbed by improper GUI behaviour.
- **Cognitive** - here we see if the user interface is sufficient to perform the test task. We are more interested in whether it will intuitively reveal (or whether its GUI itself will guide) the correct path and solve the task.

In the collaborative approach we also find the possibility of so-called pair testing [5, 6], where one task is solved by a pair of participants. Their interaction is required.

Collaborative procedures, or a mix of collaborative and classical Jacobs' Nielsen testing will allow us to answer our questions:

What is the general user friendliness of business process modelling tools BPMN [9, 10] and for example BORM [11, 22].

These questions are probably important and are waiting to be answered. One example is scientific work, which deals with the quality of process models and the implementation of DEMO methodology. Its title is: "An empirical study of the application of the DEMO method for improving BPMN process models in academia" [14]. It is clear from the authors' work that simplification of process models is desirable for many reasons. After all, we studied and presented this problem with our team last year [23]. A similar problem is currently going through conceptual modelling tools such as OntoUML [12] and UML [13].

2 Materials and Methods

In order to determine the scale which, we can determine the quality of the tool, we must define the basic attributes of the measurement. Here we suggest to inspire of the Nielsen Norman Group [15] and consider it as a crucial standard of quality of the Usability process modelling tool.

Definition of Usability [15] *"Usability is a quality attribute that assesses how easy user interfaces are to use. The word "usability" also refers to methods for improving ease-of-use during the design process"*.

Usability has 5 attributes [15]:

- **Learnability:** How easy is it for users to accomplish basic tasks the first time they encounter the design?
- **Efficiency:** Once users have learned the design, how quickly can they perform tasks?
- **Memorability:** When users return to the design after a period of not using it, how easily can they re-establish proficiency?
- **Errors:** How many errors do users make, how severe are these errors, and how easily can they recover from the errors?
- **Satisfaction:** How pleasant is it to use the design?

The Usability test [15–17] was performed according to the Collaborative Testing Guidelines [1, 17] in the Usability Lab [17] by the method of collecting defined measurement attributes. This was successfully used for the purpose of designing the quality of process models [1–7]. The usability test has also been enhanced with Eye tracking, which is currently supported by Tobii Tech [18]. The tool is part of HUBRU [17] and the results from its activities were published by J. Pavlíček, Švec et al. scientific papers [19, 20] or by the team J. Pavlíček, P. Pavlíčková at the EOMAS 2018 [23].

2.1 Laboratory Measurement Architecture

The HUBRU lab in which the measurements are made was follow the following architecture:

- Observing room

  - 4 environmental camcorders
  - 10 Pc with face camcorder, screen recording, voice recording,
  - 2 pc with eye tracking

- Control room

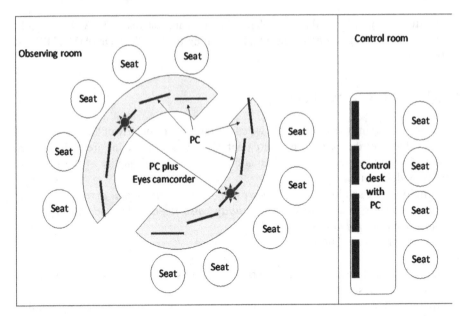

Fig. 1. Collaborative usability lab [17]

- Recorders for all pc, control monitors etc.

As can be seen from the Fig. 1, two workstations were equipped with an eye tracking system. Here it is possible to record the course of the study at the speed of tens of frames per second. Of course, the accuracy of the system depends on the original setting, but also on the actual need of the researcher or research group.

2.2 Eye Tracking System

During the workshop our team presented an eye-tracking camera system used in the study problems [1–7]. That help us to monitor the orientation of the participant's view. These results are graphically presented – Fig. 2.

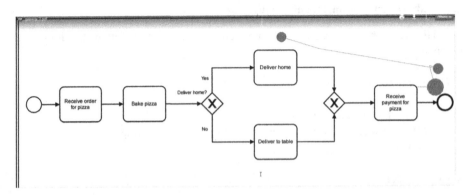

Fig. 2. Process model tracked by Eye tracking system (Color figure online)

As the sample picture shows Figs. 2 and 3, participant focuses from delivery activity to process finish and returned back into Receive payment for pizza. On this activity he spends long time (the red circle is increasing).

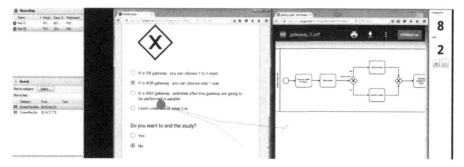

Fig. 3. Process model understanding test (Color figure online)

Of course, this model is simple, but it shows which values we can read from the concrete test. However, in previous papers [1–7] we used this tool to design process steps and the results were satisfactory [23].

Figure 3 shows the participant's concentration on the test case and its solution by reading and understanding the process model on the right side of the screen.

2.3 Usability Test

The Usability test is compound from:

1. **UI test definition** – defines study goals (to improve graphical user interface, find usability issues etc.).
2. **User groups or personas definition** – defines consumers goal of the product (User Groups – ideal for common application as internet web pages used for huge mas of the users, Personas – for deeply user focused applications as apps for mobile devices)
3. **UI test** - defines type of the usability study (heuristic or cognitive)
4. **The post–test interview** – tries to highlight findings gained during the UI Test.
5. **The usability issues definition** – defines gaps in the UI, improve recommendation etc. (Fig. 4)

3 Results

During our workshop presentation we performed Usability study for two notations (BPMN, Demo). The Usability study shows, the UX approaches are valid for evaluation the process model quality (mainly usability). The presented models Fig. 5 were tested via the Usability test methodology presented above.

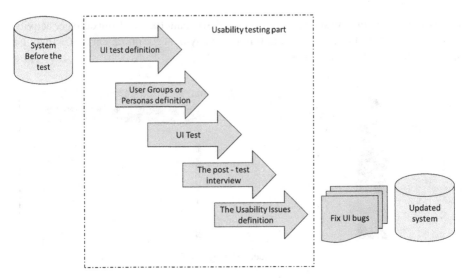

Fig. 4. Usability test steps

The important step of Usability study is to fill the questionnaire. This method helps us to recognize, if the participant's understand the process (Fig. 6).

At the end of the Usability study we performed the final interviews. During that we highlighted the observed usability issues. We gained important suggestions from the process model areas and suggestions how to improve the used methodology.

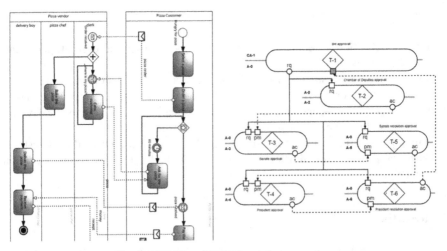

Fig. 5. BPMN and DEMO notation examples

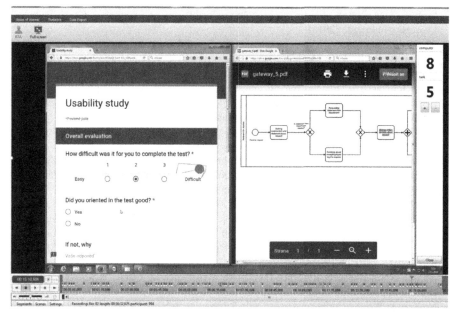

Fig. 6. The model quality verification

4 Conclusion

There have been several studies of different business models in the past, some focused-on DEMO, BORM and others on BPMN. It can be concluded from this research that there are merits and demerits to both Business Models focused on in this work. There are also some similarities between them. These demerits, merits and similarities have been expatiated above.

Overall, even based on interviews, we can state that the Usability testing method can be used to measure, evaluate and design metrics for the process model quality.

References

1. Pavlicek, J., Hronza, R., Pavlickova, P., Jelinkova, K.: The business process model quality metrics. In: Pergl, R., Lock, R., Babkin, E., Molhanec, M. (eds.) Enterprise and Organizational Modeling and Simulation. LNBIP, vol. 298, pp. 134–148. Springer, Cham (2017). https://doi.org/10.1007/978-3-319-68185-6_10. ISBN: 978-3-319-68184-9
2. Pavlicek, J., Hronza, R., Pavlickova, P.: Educational business process model skills improvement. In: Pergl, R., Molhanec, M., Babkin, E., Fosso Wamba, S. (eds.) EOMAS 2016. LNBIP, vol. 272, pp. 172–184. Springer, Cham (2016). https://doi.org/10.1007/978-3-319-49454-8_12
3. Hronza, R., Pavlíček, J., Náplava, P.: Míry kvality procesních modelů vytvořených v notaci BPMN. Acta Inform. Pragensia **4**(2), 140–153 (2015)
4. Jelínková, K.: Návrh měr kvality obchodních procesních modelů. Czech Technical University in Prague (2017)

5. Lassaková, M.: Návrh a tvorba měr pro výpočet kvality procesních modelů. Czech Technical University in Prague (2016)
6. Neumann, M.: Míry kvality procesních modelů. Czech Technical University in Prague (2016)
7. Hronza, R., Pavlíček, J., Mach, R., Náplava, P.: Míry kvality v procesním modelování. Acta Inform. Pragensia 4(1), 18–29 (2015)
8. Mach, R.: Návrh a tvorba nástroje pro optimalizaci procesů na základě analýzy BPM modelů. Czech Technical University in Prague (2015)
9. Bruce, S.: BPMN Method and Style. Cody-Cassidy Press, Aptos (2011)
10. OMG: Business Process Model & Notation (BPMN) (2016). http://www.omg.org/bpmn/index.htm. Accessed 21 Mar 2017
11. Knott, R., Merunka, V., Polak, J.: The BORM methodology: a third-generation fully object-oriented. Knowl. Based Syst. (2003). https://doi.org/10.1016/S0950-7051(02)00075-8
12. Bassetto, L.: OntoUML Specification. http://ontology.com.br/ontouml/spec/
13. OMG: Unified Modeling Language (UML) (2008). http://www.uml.org
14. Náplava, P., Pergl, R.: Empirical study of applying the demo method for improving bpmn process models in academic environment. In: Proceedings of the 17th IEEE Conference on Business Informatics, pp. 18–26. IEEE Operations Center, Piscataway (2015). ISBN: 978-1-4673-7340-1
15. Nielsen Norman Group: Evidence-Based User Experience Research. https://www.nngroup.com/
16. Nielsen, J.: Why you only need to test with 5 users. Jakob Nielsens Alertbox, vol. 19, pp. 1–4 (2000)
17. Pavlicek, J., Bock, R.: Collaborative Usability lab design and methodology to use that, part of HUBRU (2017). http://hubru.pef.czu.cz
18. Tobii Tech: Eye tracking. https://www.tobii.com/tech/technology/what-is-eye-tracking
19. Pavlicek, J., Svec, V., Pavlickova, P., Kreckova, J.: FactOrEasy© Game. In: ERIE 2016 (2016). ISBN: 978-80-213-2646-0. WOS: 000389901400056
20. Svec, V., Pavlicek, J., Ticha, I., Kreckova, J.: FactOrEasy©: art and craft of management? In: ERIE 2016 (2016). ISBN: 978-80-213-2646-0. WOS: 000389901400072
21. Nielsen, J., Mack, R.L.: Usability Inspection Methods. Wiley, New York (1994). ISBN: 0-471-01877-5
22. Merunka, V.: Object-oriented process modeling and simulation – borm experience. Trakia J. Sci. 8(8), 71–87 (2010). http://www.uni-sz.bg
23. Pavlicek, J., Pavlickova, P.: Methods for evaluating the quality of process modelling tools. In: Pergl, R., Babkin, E., Lock, R., Malyzhenkov, P., Merunka, V. (eds.) EOMAS 2018. LNBIP, vol. 332, pp. 171–177. Springer, Cham (2018). https://doi.org/10.1007/978-3-030-00787-4_12

Author Index

Printed in the United States
By Bookmasters